STICKY
CHURCH

The Leadership Network Innovation Series

The Big Idea: Focus the Message, Multiply the Impact
Dave Ferguson, Jon Ferguson, and Eric Bramlett

*Confessions of a Reformission Rev.: Hard Lessons from an
Emerging Missional Church*
Mark Driscoll

*Leadership from the Inside Out: Examining the Inner Life of a
Healthy Church Leader*
Kevin Harney

*The Multi-Site Church Revolution: Being One Church in Many
Locations*
Geoff Surratt, Greg Ligon, and Warren Bird

Other titles forthcoming

Other Books by Larry Osborne

*A Contrarian's Guide to Knowing God: Spirituality
for the Rest of Us*

Measuring Up (with Stuart Briscoe and Knute Larson)

*The Unity Factor: Developing a Healthy
Leadership Team*

STICKY
CHURCH

LARRY OSBORNE

ZONDERVAN®

ZONDERVAN.com/
AUTHORTRACKER
follow your favorite authors

ZONDERVAN®

Sticky Church
Copyright © 2008 by Larry Osborne

This title is also available as a Zondervan ebook.
Visit www.zondervan.com/ebooks.

Requests for information should be addressed to:

Zondervan, *Grand Rapids, Michigan 49530*

Library of Congress Cataloging-in-Publication Data

Osborne, Larry W., 1952–
        Sticky church / Larry Osborne.
                p. cm. – (The leadership network innovation series)
        Includes bibliographical references.
        ISBN 978-0-310-28508-3 (softcover)
        1. Church growth. 2. Church group work. 3. Small groups – Religious
aspects – Christianity. 4. North Coast Church (San Diego County, Calif.) I. Title.
BV652.25.O83 2008
253 – dc22 2008021323

Interior design by Matthew Van Zomeren

Printed in the United States of America

---

10 11 12 13 14 • 23 22 21 20 19 18 17 16 15 14 13 12 11

Contents

Contents

Part 1

THE
STICKY
CHURCH
ADVANTAGE

Chapter 1

Sticky Church

If the back door of a church is left wide open, it doesn't matter how many people are coaxed to come in the front door—or the side door, for that matter.

Yet most churches give the back door scant attention.

We've discovered lots of ways to reach people. We've offered the high-powered programs and slick marketing of attractional churches, the cultural savvy of missional churches, and the relational intimacy of small churches. But we've often become so focused on *reaching* people that we've forgotten the importance of *keeping* people.

And that's the thesis of this book: Our churches need to be stickier.

Stickier churches are healthier churches. They not only draw in spiritual window-shoppers and lead them to Christ; they also grow them up to maturity.

And that, after all, is what Jesus called us to do. He didn't tell us to go into all the world and sign people up. He didn't tell us to draw big crowds. He told us to make disciples—a task that includes baptizing people *and* teaching them to obey *everything* he commanded.[1]

Frankly, that's a task that takes some significant time. To pull it off, we need to be sticky.

Why Stickiness Is So Important

In one of Jesus' most famous parables, the parable of the sower, he told of a farmer casting seeds onto four types of soil, each representing a different response to the gospel.[2]

One of the soils was so hard that nothing could germinate.

Another was so shallow that the plants sprouted quickly but couldn't dig their roots deep enough to withstand the furnace blast of a Middle Eastern summer's day.

The third kind of soil was weed infested, resulting in a crop that once again looked good for a while but eventually was choked off by what Jesus called the deceitfulness of riches and the desire for other things.

Only the fourth type of soil, the one Jesus called the good soil, produced a harvest.

Now, the point of this parable is straightforward: A great spiritual start is no guarantee of a happy ending.

But somehow many of us have missed it.

Just look at the way we typically respond to a burst of church growth or the baby steps of a new believer. We're quick to rejoice at the first signs of spiritual life—and rightfully so. But in most cases, while we hope that the growth lasts and continues, the sprouting of the seed is the main thing. That's what we count; that's what we celebrate.

If the seed dries up and dies at the first sign of hardship, we're bummed. But we're hardly devastated. At least it sprouted and popped out of the ground—and that's a lot better than never having started at all.

The same goes for anyone who starts out well and lasts for a while before being choked off by the weeds of worldly concern. We wish it hadn't happened. We wanted better for them. But at least they got off to a good start.

Here's the problem. Unlike Jesus' original audience, few of us know much about farming. For most of us, the produce aisle is a close encounter with agriculture. So we completely miss the emotional response that anyone raised on a farm would have had to this parable.

No farmer would ever be satisfied with initial growth killed off before harvest. If the soil in any portion of his field produced that result, he'd never plant there again.

A crop that didn't last all the way to harvest was a financial disaster. The response wouldn't be a shrug and an "Oh well." It would be more akin to sackcloth and ashes.

I realize that most scholars see the soil in this parable as representing the condition of individual hearts—and I agree. But the underlying principles are not only true for individuals; they are also true for the ministry of a local church.

I also realize that this passage could easily springboard us into a centuries-old debate about eternal security. But that's not my point or within the scope of this book. Wherever you personally land on that one, the question of the day remains the same: What does Jesus' parable about the four soils have to say about the way we do church?

To my thinking it says a lot. And one of the most important things it says about our churches is that stickiness matters.

The Purpose of This Book

Don't take what I've said to mean that I'm against trying to open the front door wider. I'm not. I'd like to open it as wide as possible. It's just that I've learned that if left alone, the back door never closes itself. We have to intentionally slam it shut.

In the following pages we'll explore how to do that. We'll see what makes a church sticky, from its values and priorities to its structures, programs, and practices.

In particular we'll look in depth at sermon-based small groups, a lecture-lab model for studying the weekend sermon in-depth during the week. We'll see how they work. We'll explain why they have the power to make your church especially sticky. And we'll discover why so many of the traditional small group models we've tried in the past sound great but don't work all that well in real life.

My goal is to provide you with a working model that you can adopt and change until it's ready to be put into play in your unique ministry setting.

I've deliberately written in a conversational tone. I hope you'll feel like we're hanging out, discussing the ins and outs of ministry, sipping a latte at our favorite gathering place. I'll tell you my story. You decide what works for you and what doesn't.

Much of this story will be told through the lens of North Coast Church, located in a suburb north of San Diego. Since 1980 I've had the privilege of pastoring an amazing group of people who've been willing to innovate but also — perhaps more important — abandon programs and traditions that no longer work.

That means that these insights, programs, and principles have all been hammered out on the anvil of local church ministry, not only at North Coast Church but also in the many churches that have already adopted their own version of sermon-based small groups.

And unlike many books on ministry, this isn't the result of a rush to publish. It's not about the newest "next big thing." It's not based on an unproven track record of two or three years. It's the result of decades of successes, failures, refinements, and midcourse corrections.

Even more important, these principles scale. They (and the sermon-based small group model) worked just as well when we were a small church of less than two hundred adults as they do today in a multisite megachurch with more than seven thousand in weekend attendance.

They've also proven to be transferable to a wide array of theological, denominational, and cultural backgrounds. They've helped close the back door in small, large, rural, suburban, and urban churches — as well as edgy churches and traditional churches.

The reason is quite simple. The need for stickiness is universal. The details of how we get there will vary from ministry to ministry. But the broad-brush principles are strikingly similar in every situation.

Here's an interesting scenario for you to ponder. Imagine two churches that each grew in attendance from 250 people to 500 over a ten-year period.

Church A is a revolving door. It loses 7 people for every 10 it adds. To reach 500, it will have to add 834 new members or attenders.

Church B is a sticky church. It loses only 3 people for every 10 it adds. To reach 500, it has to add 357 new members or attenders.

On the surface, both churches appear to have doubled. But the revolving door church had to reach 834 new people to get there, while the sticky church only needed to reach 357.

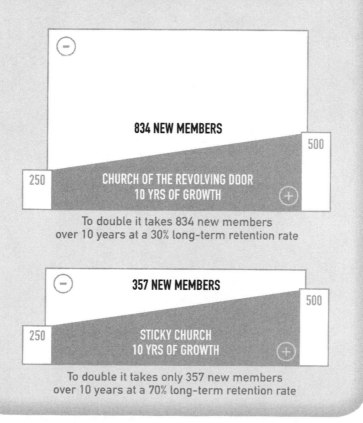

834 NEW MEMBERS

500

250   CHURCH OF THE REVOLVING DOOR
10 YRS OF GROWTH

To double it takes 834 new members
over 10 years at a 30% long-term retention rate

357 NEW MEMBERS

500

250   STICKY CHURCH
10 YRS OF GROWTH

To double it takes only 357 new members
over 10 years at a 70% long-term retention rate

Obviously, doubling attendance is a lot easier for the sticky church than for the revolving door church. No surprise there. But here's the kicker: *After ten years, the church with the big back door will have 500 attenders* and *584 former attenders!* And every year after that, the spread between the number of ex-attenders and the number of current attenders will grow larger.

No matter what that church does to expand the size of the front door, it's going to be hard to keep reaching people when the predominant word on the street is, "I *used* to go there."

Chapter 2

Who Are These Guys?

If I'm going to tell you what we've done, you have a right to know who we are. So here's the North Coast story. When it comes to marketing and advertising, we stink. Almost all of our growth has come by word of mouth. That helps explain why and how stickiness became so important to our ministry. But here's the rest of the story.

When I first came to North Coast, we were a small church meeting in an old high school cafeteria. I hadn't been there long when someone showed me an advertisement we were putting in the local newspaper each weekend. You know the drill: We were supposedly the friendliest church in town, with great preaching, great worship, and a world-class children's program.

The truth was, we had none of those things. Not even close. I'm not sure I would have kept coming if I hadn't been the pastor.

The cafeteria was old and smelly. Remnants of food fights hung from the wall. One whole side of the room was a large Plexiglas window, which was cool — except when skateboarders started showing off in the middle of a sermon. That was hard to compete with. Most of the time they'd win. They were a lot more interesting than my early sermons. They'd probably still be more interesting. That's one reason we moved.

So I did the only reasonable thing. I canceled the ad. I had enough issues on my hands. I didn't need the Federal Communications Commission hassling me for false advertising.

From that point on, outside of a small listing in the yellow pages, we've never marketed or advertised. We've not held any special evangelistic weekends where people were asked to bring their friends. We've not even used the free advertising that some organizations offer churches for Easter and Christmas Eve.

That's not to say I'm against marketing. Not in the least. We might do it someday. But to this point, we've opted to close the back door and grow by word of mouth, in the belief that even a small trickle can flood the whole house if everything is locked up tight.

Slamming the Back Door Shut

Basically, what we've done is to take most of the energy and resources we would have spent on special programming and front-door events and instead poured it into making our church more welcoming and sticky.

Rather than trying to have the most creative sermon series, the hippest worship, the best dog and pony show on Easter or Christmas Eve, we've simply tried to serve our people so well that they'll want to bring their friends, without needing to be asked to do so.

Everything we do is aimed at helping the Christians we already have grow stronger in Christ. But everything is done in such a way that their non-Christian friends will understand all that we're saying and doing. Bottom line: We've tried to create a perfect storm for come-and-see evangelism while velcroing newcomers for long-term spiritual growth.

I'm not saying we never have people walk out the back door. Of course we do. And sometimes it's more than a few — usually over some great theological issue like allowing coffee in the sanctuary, changing the worship style, or using the subwoofers at full capacity.

But historically our back door has been so small that still today if someone leaves for reasons other than moving, it will usually be on the agenda in one of our senior staff meetings.

The 80 Percent Factor

By far the most powerful tool for keeping our back door shut and making the church sticky has been our commitment to sermon-based small groups.

In fact, the most important number to know about North Coast Church is not the weekend attendance. It's the percentage of adults who participate in one of our small groups.

Since 1985 that number has equaled at least 80 percent of our average weekend attendance.

Let me explain how we arrive at that number. My bet is that many of you are as suspect of small group numbers as I am. Besides the usual evangelistic exaggeration, it seems to me that most of the time what's reported is the number of people who *signed up* to be in a small group, not the number who actually come.

I've had friends tell me that thousands are in their small group ministry. But when I go snoop around to discover how they do it, more often than not I find they aren't doing it. But they sure did have great sign-ups.

To keep ourselves honest and to give ourselves an accurate benchmark to compare with year after year, we use the following formula to determine how many are in our groups.

First, we only count groups that meet under the umbrella of our small group ministry. Like any church, we have lots of folks who meet in other settings: accountability groups, service groups, Bible studies, and the like. But we don't count them, because we have no accurate way to keep track of what's going on or the ebb and flow of who's involved and who's dropped out.

To determine our percentage in small groups, we take the average weekend adult attendance in the month of October and figure out what 80 percent of that number is. Then we check to see how many people are in our growth groups (the name we use for our organized small groups). For us, this number should equal or exceed the 80 percent figure every year. So far it has.

Occasionally, we've temporarily slipped below the 80 percent mark (and I'm sure we will again someday). Each time, it has called for an all-hands-on-deck meeting. Since we see these groups as the hub of our ministry — more important than even the weekend services — we've stopped to figure out what went wrong and how to fix it. Each time, we were back above 80 percent by the next quarter.

Now, I don't know what your ideal small group percentage should be. We certainly don't think 80 percent is any sort of sacred number. It's just our number.

Every church and every community is different. A low number in one setting might be amazingly healthy in another. For instance, churches with a long history of adult Sunday school will always have a lower percentage of small group involvement than churches where small groups are the only option for fellowship and growth. It's not a matter of spirituality; it's a matter of competition for time and resources.

Scalability

Many programs and concepts work well at one size but fall apart with growth. One of my greatest surprises has been how easily sermon-based small groups have adapted as we've grown. If you would have asked me in the early 1990s if I thought we could still use the same primary tools to keep the back door shut in a so-called megachurch that we did when we were a few hundred, I would have said, "No way." But I was wrong.

I would have assumed that the anonymity of a larger church and the complexity of a multisite, multiple venue ministry would have called for something different. But they haven't.

The same principles that made us sticky at two hundred and four hundred have kept us sticky at thousands. The same emphasis that made us healthy as a small church — our focus on closing the back door and velcroing people to sermon-based small groups — has kept us healthy as a large church.

Slow Growth

Along with scalability, it's probably important to point out one more thing. I've noticed over the years that once North Coast Church became large and well known, there were some folks who immediately wrote off anything we said about ministry as only applying to a megachurch.

It's as if they assumed that North Coast was always a big church—or at least became one overnight.

Not so. As we'll see in the next chapter, North Coast grew quite slowly in the early days. It took five years to go from 130 to 180. It took another five years to reach 750.

I know what it's like to be my own secretary, to stuff the bulletins, to wonder if we'll ever break the 200 barrier. And lucky for me, I also know what it's like to have a marvelous staff that makes me look a lot better and wiser than I really am. If I were forced to choose between the two scenarios, you probably know which one I'd pick. But I have seen and known both.

Most important, the principles in this book have served me well in both settings. And I'm confident that they'll serve you just as well.

Chapter 3

How I Learned about the Importance and Power of Stickiness

I always look back on 1980 to 1983 as the Dark Years. They weren't particularly tough in anything that really matters. I had good health, a great wife, a new son, an excellent walk with God.

But my ministry sucked.

I'd come to San Diego filled with dreams and zeal to do great things for God. I was only twenty-eight. But I'd had great success in two previous churches where I'd served as a youth pastor. I thought I was one of the lucky ones, blessed with a ministry Midas touch. I figured it would be only a matter of time until our little church became a huge church.

But within weeks the wheels began to fall off. I quickly discovered that this pastoring gig (even in a church much smaller than my youth groups) was a lot tougher than it looked from a distance.

I'd been oblivious to the fact that I'd always built on someone else's foundation. I'd started one college group from scratch and resurrected another from the dead, but the churches themselves were relatively large, providing me with a great fishing pool from which to find leaders and potential students.

Now I was on my own. No underpinning, no well-stocked fishing pools—just a cruddy office in the garage of a generous parishioner and a stinky old cafeteria with food fights and skateboarders.

Killing the Dream

We did have some quick initial growth. On my "candidating" Sunday—basically a dog and pony show where you preach your best sermon and then hope the congregation votes to have you come and preach your not-so-great sermons—128 people showed up.

Within weeks we'd jumped up to 150.

Three years later we had climbed all the way to 151—a growth rate of one-third of a person per year! Most of the time we hovered around 135, which means we were actually going backward.

So one day I decided to do something I never thought I'd do. I killed the dream.

I'd always been big on having clear and well-defined dreams. So much so that I had a little notebook that spelled out in great detail the house we'd live in someday, the career and mommy track my wife would take, the investments we'd make, when and how I would write, and so on. Included was a page that described pastoring a church of one thousand or more.

It was obvious that we'd never get there at a growth rate of one person every three years. So I opened my notebook, took out the "pastor a big church" page, and threw it away. I figured that I'd badly overestimated my potential. If I didn't have the horsepower to pull it off, I didn't want to keep living with the pressure of trying to pull it off.

The emotional release was amazing. No longer saddled with an unrealistic dream of growing a big church, I started to relax and enjoy the ministry I already had.

At the time, I thought I'd buried a dream. But now, looking back, I realize that in reality I'd taken my first small step toward creating a truly sticky church. That's because once I gave up the dream of reaching everyone outside the church, I was suddenly free to focus on taking care of those who were already inside the church.

Tools or Sheep?

I hate to admit it. But before I killed the dream, I wasn't dialed in on tending the flock God had entrusted to me. Instead, to be brutally honest, I was using the people I already had to reach the people I wanted to reach. They weren't sheep to be cared for; they were tools to be utilized. And while I doted on every new person who came through the front door, more and more were walking out the back door.

I know that sounds crass, unspiritual, and pretty lame for a pastor to admit. But it's true. Sadly true. And what's worse, I'm not alone.

I've noticed over the years that it's become increasingly fashionable for pastors in churches with a strong evangelistic or innovative bent (among whom I count myself) to claim that they don't like to be around Christians.

One pastor recently told me that he didn't want any Christians coming to his new church plant. He only wanted non-Christians searching for God, and new Christians who'd recently come to Christ.

On one hand, I understand where he's coming from. He's tired of dealing with small-minded traditionalists who want to maintain a historical preservation society more than fulfill the mission.

But on the other hand, I fear for the unintended consequences of his outlook. If he's only going to reach out to non-Christians and nurture new Christians, what's he going to do when those new Christians become plain ol' Christians, the kind he hates to be around?

His patience and compassion flow easily toward people caught in the addictive clutches of sin. He thinks the rough language and butchered theology of a new Christian is cool, sort of like the cute things little kids say and do. But two or three years later his patience runs thin and the compassion runs dry when he realizes that these cute new Christians are still dealing with the same old issues.

At that point he leaves the "slow growers" to fend for themselves. Many quietly make their way out the back door, though he never seems to notice in the excitement of all the new folks coming through the front door.

There's another large group of churches at the opposite end of the spectrum. These are the ingrown and dying churches that don't seem to care if anyone ever comes through the front door—or goes to hell, for that matter.

On the surface, they can appear to be focused on one another and somewhat sticky, but they're not. Ingrown and dying churches don't take care of the flock. They appease the flock. And they're not very sticky either. Except for a small group of people welded tightly together at the center, these churches are a lot more like teflon than velcro. Just try to connect with one. You can't unless you're willing to marry a member's daughter.

Putting the First Thing First

The decision to focus on the people I already had helped to close the back door. The decision to stop advertising forced us to grow by word of mouth. The end result was not only an exponential increase in our ability to hold on to the people we already had but also a huge increase in our ability to reach and keep new people.

I now realize that's because people who come through the front door of a church through word-of-mouth referrals have a fundamentally different experience than do those who come as the result of a marketing campaign.

When it comes to reaching and keeping people, word-of-mouth churches have some significant advantages. In the next chapter, we'll examine three of these advantages in depth. But first I need to reiterate that I'm not against marketing. This is not an anti-marketing or anti-special-programs book. It's a pro-stickiness book.

Marketing and special programs are great outreach tools, especially if we've closed the back door and aligned what people actually experience with what we promise. But having said that, I do believe we often start our marketing and outreach campaigns too soon.

Imagine a restaurant that kicks off with splashy mailers and hands out tons of coupons before making sure the kitchen and waitstaff have their act together. Sure, lots of people will come to check it out, but if the meals are pedestrian and the staff is barely competent, not many will come back again—ever. Even if things eventually turn around, it's unlikely that more coupons or even a few word-of-mouth recommendations will overcome the initial negative experience for those early customers. They weren't reached; they were inoculated.

In a similar vein, a church that developes a ministry worthy of word-of-mouth referrals before launching its marketing campaigns or outreach programs will find that those who come once the marketing begins won't just pop in for a quick look—they'll stick around for the long haul.

That doesn't mean we all have to become a "high buzz" church or offer the top-notch programs or staffing of a megachurch. McDonald's doesn't try to be Ruth's Chris Steak House. Each has its own niche. One reaches those who want or need a cheap meal for the kids. The other serves those who are looking for a sizzling fillet. Each has its raving fans.

In the same way, some folks love the wow of a big church. Some love the intimacy of a small church. Many find the in-between size of a midsized church (big enough for critical mass, small enough to need everyone) to be just right.

What matters is not the size of the church or the slickness of the programming. What matters is that those who come find a ministry and relationships worthy of spontaneous word-of-mouth recommendations.

When that happens, a church is primed to hold on to the people it already has *and* the people they bring with them.

Three Big Changes

When I started focusing on closing the back door instead of widening the front door, it led to three major changes.

First, it changed the way I related to our lay leadership team. When most of my focus was on getting more people through the front door, the inner workings and interpersonal relationships of the board seemed more like a nuisance than an important part of our ministry.

But a sticky church needs a healthy leadership team composed of people who genuinely like one another, share the same vision, and pull in the same direction. It's hard to close the back door when everyone is headed a different direction or there's an undercurrent of distrust and conflict. And if board members leave the church once their term is up, it's pretty tough to close the back door for everyone else.[*]

The second big change was in the way I taught and led our congregation. Focusing on the front door aimed everything at two kinds of people: the not-yet Christian or the super saint who was ready to help me charge the hill. There wasn't much room for people who came to Christ but didn't grow at a fast enough pace or carried lots of old baggage.

Closing the back door meant finding a way to help these people discover a path to spirituality that worked for them, one that would enable them to finish the race — not by excusing sin but by accommodating their slower pace.[**]

The third change involved launching a small group ministry focused primarily on building significant relationships rather than growing the church. The new groups we started soon morphed into the sermon-based small groups that we'll look at more closely later.

Almost immediately we became a noticeably stickier and healthier church. The back door slammed shut, and to my surprise more people than ever began coming through the front door.

[*] For more on this, see Larry Osborne, *The Unity Factor: Developing a Healthy Leadership Team*, 4th ed. (Vista, CA: Owl's Nest, 2006); www.northcoastchurch.com.

[**] For more on this, see Larry Osborne, *A Contrarian's Guide to Knowing God: Spirituality for the Rest of Us* (Colorado Springs, CO: Multnomah, 2007).

Chapter 4

Why Stickier Churches Are Healthier Churches

We've already seen that sticky churches have an advantage when it comes to discipleship. Shutting the back door gives them more time to grow people to full maturity. But they also have an advantage when it comes to outreach.

Ultimately, a church grows in one of two ways: It gets more people to come through the front door, or it stops losing people out the back door. While most churches give lip service to the importance of both, in reality there's usually a strong bias toward one or the other—and in most cases it's not too hard to tell which one it is.

Front-door churches tend to look for the newest and best ways to be noticed and bring people in. If you could be a fly on the wall at an evaluation meeting, you'd find most of the discussion centered on how many people came to the big event.

Sticky churches might have great marketing and incredible programs, but if you could be a fly on the wall at their evaluation meeting, you'd find a different discussion. Instead of celebrating how many people came, the most important measurement would be how many came back.

While many would assume that a church focused on bringing people in the front door would have an advantage when it comes to reaching the lost, that's not necessarily true over the long haul. Churches that close the back door effectively do so by serving their congregations so well that the people don't want to leave. And happy sheep are incurable word-of-mouth marketers.

Whether it's the fabulous food at our favorite restaurant, the excitement of a great movie, or the life-changing impact of a church ministry, most of us can't help but tell others when we've been well served—and no one needs to tell us to do so.

First Visits

There is a fundamental difference between someone whose first visit to a church is the result of a powerful marketing campaign or a special outreach program and someone whose first trip is the result of a friend's invitation to a regular service.

People who come because of special marketing or programming walk in expecting (or hoping) to be wowed. And if they are, they come back expecting more of the same.

But of course that's not what they get, because special programs are—well, special. They might attract a lot of people; they might deeply touch everyone who comes. But in the end they fly in the face of one of the most basic laws of retention: *Whatever you do to reach people you have to continue to do to keep them.*

Let's think through the experience of an unchurched neighbor who decides to come to a special outreach event. Suppose he likes it well enough to come back the next week. When he does, the exceptional music, the props, the great speaker, or whatever else it was that duly impressed him will almost surely be gone. If it's the weekend after Christmas or Easter, it's likely that the senior pastor and all the folks who put it together will be gone also. After all, they'll need a break. It's not easy to put on such an extravaganza.

Now compare that with the neighbor whose first visit is the result of a word-of-mouth invitation to a typical weekend service. While he might not be as impressed or wowed by the initial show, he certainly won't be as disappointed when he shows up a second time. There's no bait and switch to overcome. If he liked the first visit well enough to come back a second time, he's likely to come back a third and fourth time as well.

But that's not all. A word-of-mouth church also has some significant advantages when it comes to evangelism, follow-up, and assimilation.

Natural Evangelism

Perhaps the most common form of natural evangelism is what I like to call come-and-see evangelism. It takes place whenever someone shares a spiritual need or interest and we respond by inviting him or her to come to a Bible study, to attend a church service, or just to hang out with some of our Christian friends.

It gives that person an opportunity to see Christianity and Christians up close and personal. It's low-threat. There's seldom any pressure. It lets spiritual window-shoppers move toward Jesus at a Spirit-led pace. It's completely natural, not forced.

Let's face it: Most Christians are pretty lame when it comes to closing the deal evangelistically. Whether it's aggressive confrontational witnessing or low-key friendship evangelism, lots of us don't know what to say or do when the questions get tough.

Even when someone is obviously ready to step over the line and follow Jesus, many of us still stutter and stammer or shift into automatic pilot as we spout off a poorly memorized and highly canned response.

I'm not saying that's a good thing or a bad thing. I am saying that's the way it is. Even those of us who are extroverts with lots of training in evangelism can get tongue-tied and sweaty palms.

But a sticky church offers the perfect environment for come-and-see evangelism, because while every service is designed to help Christians become better Christians, it is always done in a way that non-Christians can understand everything that's said and takes place.

That makes it much easier for even the most introverted and reserved among us to say with confidence when a friend or coworker expresses a spiritual interest or need, "Why don't you just come and see?"

Contrast that with the way many of our front-door churches approach evangelism. Though we might think that our special programs make it easier for members to reach out to their not-yet-Christian friends, our special outreach programs can actually put some obstacles in their way.

The first is timing. High-powered front-door programs can have the unintended consequence of sending a message that some weekends and programs are for bringing guests—and the rest aren't.

Years ago my parents had some friends whom they hoped to reach for Christ. After numerous dinner conversations and plenty of time to watch how my folks lived and dealt with life's thorny issues, the husband, seemingly out of the blue, said that he and his wife would love to come to church sometime.

Needless to say, my dad and mom were delighted. The Sunday service started out with a great worship set. Then the smiley guy got up to give some commercials and take the offering right before the sermon, which, judging by its title on the bulletin, looked like a great one. So far, so good.

Then it happened. Smiley guy began to wax eloquent about an upcoming outreach event that would be the perfect opportunity to bring an "unsaved" friend. Special flyers and brochures were available in the back to pick up and hand out. He then encouraged everyone to be sure they were praying for their lost friends. As he went on and on, my dad and mom slowly died. So did their "unsaved" friends, who had made the mistake of wanting to come to church a couple of weeks too soon.

They never did come back.

My parents learned an important lesson: Never bring friends who don't know Jesus to the wrong service.

Though my folks no longer go to that church, I observed it long enough to see that lots of others got the same message. Special programs always brought in a large crowd. But no one seemed to notice how few returned or how well the entire congregation had been trained to hold back their invitations until the next big event.

Now, here's the irony. All this happened at a self-proclaimed "seeker church."

There is a second unintended obstacle that highly programmed front-door churches can put in the way of natural evangelism. If most of the people who come to Christ come as the result of a complex and high-powered event, it sends a subtle message that it takes lots of time, planning, and money to lead someone to Christ. And that tells the average Joe to hold off until we've scheduled the next great fishing party.

That's not to say that special-event evangelism doesn't work or that those who come to Christ as a result never stick. But it seems to me that spiritual birth is a lot like physical birth. It's much easier when it's natural. Artificial insemination and other medical marvels can produce real children who grow up to have great lives, but it's a rather inefficient way to replenish the next generation.

Natural Follow-Up

Another area where a sticky church has an advantage is in following up on those who visit.

After a big event, it's hard to follow up if you don't know who came. Most people who come as a result of an advertising campaign won't readily give out their name and contact information. We've come to value privacy too much to do so.

Even at weekend services, a front-door church can have a harder time with follow-up. That's because in any church with two or more services, it's hard to tell who is a guest and who just changed services for the weekend. Since longtime members who switch services don't like to be asked if they're visiting (try it; you'll enjoy the dirty looks), most of us learn to treat anyone we don't recognize as a regular we haven't met or someone whose face we can't remember.

It's different in a sticky church. Since it doesn't place much emphasis on big front-door events, most guests are brought on the arm of a friend. Few come with only a postcard or brochure in hand.

That makes follow-up natural and more likely to occur. Friends don't need a follow-up program to remind them to ask, "How'd you like it? Any questions I can answer? Do you want to come again?" That's what friends do.

At North Coast we didn't have (or need) an organized follow-up procedure until we were well past three thousand in weekend attendance. And we only needed it then because the small percentage of folks who came alone at that point added up to a large enough number that some were falling through the cracks.

Natural Assimilation

Sticky churches have still another advantage. Since they fill the front door primarily with people who've come through word-of-mouth referrals, assimilation takes place naturally. Friends don't have to be reminded to assimilate friends. They do so naturally—and enthusiastically.

It's also easier to assimilate when there's no need to build a bridge between the bells and whistles of a big event and the more pedestrian programming of a weekend service. Even if there is an occasional measure of bait and switch, those who come by the word-of-mouth invitation of a friend will know what to expect. There'll be no surprises.

Instead of complex assimilation programs, a sticky church simply needs to provide plenty of ministry on-ramps to which members can easily connect the friends they've invited.

Why do lots of front-door churches start out fast and then suddenly stall out?

As long as the front door remains larger than the back door, any church will appear to be growing. But sooner or later the front door can't get any larger; either the budget or the skill set runs thin.

When that happens, leadership teams typically begin to do some serious soul-searching. They wonder what happened, how a dynamic, growing ministry could abruptly falter and turn into a revolving door.

In reality not much changed. The back door was always large, but as long as more people were coming in the front than going out the back, no one seemed to care.

As long as the front door is bigger than the back door - a church will think it is growing.

This seems to happen at fairly predictable sizes, the difference owing mostly to the gifting and budget of a particular church.

Some strong front-door churches get off to an impressive start before stalling out at around four hundred people. Others bounce between eight hundred and twelve hundred, with periodic growth spurts inevitably followed by a slow decline. They

When the front door and the back door can't be
opened any wider - a church stops growing.

remind me of a slow leak in a bicycle tire. You pump it up and
figure you're ready to ride, only to come back tomorrow and
find it's gone flat again.

More than a few times, I've watched a church with very
gifted communicators and artists, coupled with great marketing, hit a much higher ceiling—somewhere between twenty-
five hundred and three thousand—before its leaders started to
notice that the back door had turned the church into a revolving door.

But no matter at what size a church discovers it can't open
the front door any wider, the core issue is always the same.
Proficiency in opening the front door tends to blind us to any
growing problems at the back door. And by the time we notice,
it's often a huge hole that can't be closed easily.

Part 2

HOW
SMALL
GROUPS
CHANGE
EVERYTHING

 Chapter 5

Velcroed for Growth

Most of our discipleship programs are very linear. Unfortunately, most spiritual growth is not.

Look back at your own spiritual journey. My bet is that it was pretty haphazard. It was probably more like a meandering path than anything close to a straight line. For most of us, it would be nearly impossible to duplicate the curriculum of our life.

Yet, like many, I was weaned on a linear, step-by-step discipleship model. I attended a new believers' class designed to teach the basics of theology and how to develop a personal walk with God. (Apparently, every new Christian needed a good grasp of the Trinity, the inspiration of Scripture, the basics of the atonement, the sovereignty of God, and a few other things I can't remember.) And oh yeah, we also needed to learn how to share our faith and get started with a personal quiet time.

Though it had almost nothing to do with the stuff new Christians actually struggle with — casting aside sinful habits and cleaning up our act — we were provided with a classy binder to put our notes in.

Once we'd hung around too long to be called new Christians anymore, we were expected to work our way through a series of classes, programs, and training designed to pass along key skills and basic theology. For those of us who wanted to become pros, it all culminated with a seminary degree.

It was a slick process. It made sense on a flowchart. It was relatively easy to administer. It had a fairly high compliance rate. And it had little to nothing to do with how we actually grew.

Growth Points

Most spiritual growth doesn't come as a result of a training program or a set curriculum. It comes as a result of life putting us in what I like to call a need-to-know or need-to-grow situation.

Though the lessons we must all learn are pretty universal, the order in which we learn them and the classroom God uses to teach them are seldom the same for any two people.

Need-to-know moments happen when we find ourselves in a predicament where we need to know God's viewpoint on an issue we've never dealt with before.

For instance, imagine a dicey ethical issue at work. Perhaps you've discovered that everyone else in your office or industry winks at something you see as unethical. At that point, you need to know, "Does the Bible speak to this issue? And if so, what does it say?"

Or maybe your next-door neighbor has started to meet with some Mormon missionaries and wants you to join in. Suddenly the deity of Christ, the Trinity, the atonement, and a host of other theological issues no longer seem so dry and academic.

Need-to-grow moments are similar, but they're usually accompanied by a tough trial or a stretching experience. It might be a new job with a jerk boss, the rough sledding of a financial mess, or the pain of a broken heart. Each in its own way calls for a deeper and more obedient walk with God.

Unfortunately, our typical linear discipleship models don't handle this kind of randomness very well. They seem to be designed with the assumption that knowledge and character can be inventoried and stored up for later use. Take good notes now, because someday you'll really need this stuff!

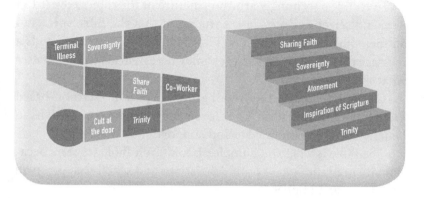

But that's not how most of us learn or change. We all learn best when we understand why a topic is important, and we change best—well, when we have to.

Velcroed for Growth

Sermon-based small groups take this haphazard learning-and-growing process into account. They're perfectly fitted to the way spiritual growth actually takes place.

The focus of a sermon-based small group is not so much on the curriculum as it is on the process. There is no set body of information that must be covered in a particular order. The topic in any one week simply flows out of whatever was taught in the previous weekend's sermon.

The ultimate goal of a sermon-based small group is simply to velcro people to the two things they will need most when faced with a need-to-know or need-to-grow situation: the Bible and other Christians.

On the one hand, the "sermon-based" aspect of these groups guarantees that the Bible remains close at hand. It really doesn't matter if some sermons are home runs and some are duds. The simple process of handling the Scriptures on a regular basis and looking into them to see what they say sets the stage for future need-to-know or need-to-grow moments.

In fact, the seemingly arbitrary nature of the topics covered in weekend sermons drives home the point that the Bible speaks to an incredible array of subjects. This apparent randomness sends a message that God has an answer somewhere in his Word, no matter what situation we face.

On the other hand, the "small group" aspect of a sermon-based group guarantees that we'll be close enough to other Christians to benefit from their knowledge and support.

The Bible is a big and complex book. Even Bible scholars occasionally need the help of other Christians and scholars to grasp all that it says and implies.

While it's true that a Lone Ranger can learn a lot through self-study, Lone Rangers (and even Brains on a Stick who know the Bible inside out) aren't exempt from need-to-know and need-to-grow moments. Yet when they are faced with one, their isolation guarantees that the only thing they'll know is what they already know.

As for wise counsel, a warm hug, or a swift kick in the rear, those are rather hard to self-administer. If we don't already have those kinds of relationships in place, it's usually too late to pull them together once a need-to-know or need-to-grow crisis hits with full force.

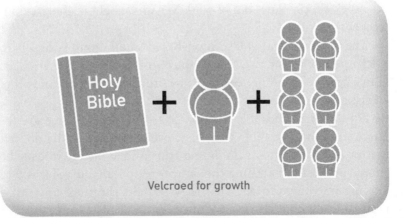

Velcroed for growth

Small Churches or Small Groups?

Whenever I speak on the importance of small groups and the need to be tightly velcroed to other Christians and the Bible, I'm asked, "If small groups are so essential to spiritual growth and a healthy ministry, why aren't they mentioned in the New Testament?" Or better yet, "Why aren't they commanded?"

My answer is that they weren't needed. When the New Testament was written, the typical church was so small that it was, in essence, a small group. Almost all of the New Testament churches met in a home. All of the values and benefits that a small group brings, they already had in place.

Some people point to this and make the claim that a small church is therefore inherently better, more biblical. Some go so far as to call for a return to house churches as the only way to return to New Testament Christianity.

Their rationale goes something like this: If it was good enough for the New Testament apostles, it ought to be good enough for us. If they changed the world with small, mostly house churches, we can too.

But their argument carries a fatal flaw. It's the assumption that New Testament churches remained small and met in homes as a ministry strategy. In other words, the apostles did it because they thought it was the best way to do church.

The truth is, they had no other choice. Without automobiles or mass transit, everything in their culture was small and neighborhood based. It wasn't a better option. It was the only option.

In addition, the early church was often a persecuted minority without social standing, wealth, or the ability to build and own a meeting hall. So it should be no surprise that most New Testament churches met in homes—and later catacombs.

But we no longer live in that world. And we haven't for centuries. Throughout history the church has continued to morph and take on new forms (while mostly staying faithful to its eternal biblical functions) as it has moved from country to country and culture to culture. And it will continue to do so until Jesus returns.

In the meantime it makes sense to structure our modern-day churches and ministries in a way that best fits how we as individuals grow spiritually.

Structured for Spiritual Growth

To be structured for spiritual growth, a church (whether front-door or back-door focused) must have some sort of method in place to consistently connect people to both significant relationships and the Bible.

In a very small church, that might be nothing more than the weekly worship gathering. But in any church of more than eighty to ninety people, it takes a plan or it won't happen.

Front-door churches that fail to structure for spiritual growth risk becoming merely a birthing center, the telltale mark of which is a back door fueled by maturity migration—a steady flow of people who complain, "I got started here, but I can't grow here."

Back-door churches that fail to structure for spiritual growth will end up with programs and ministries that keep people from leaving but do nothing to help them grow or reach out to those who need Jesus.

To combat that, the simplest and best tool I've ever seen for connecting people to one another and engaging them with the Bible for the long haul is a sermon-based small group. It offers a format that fits the way we spiritually grow, while providing a framework for a healthy and sticky church. Nothing compares.

Chapter 6

How Small Groups Change Everything

Lots of churches have small groups. But if truth be known, they're usually more of an add-on than a churchwide priority, a little something extra for those who want to go deeper with God.

While many church leaders claim that small groups are an integral part of their ministry, I've learned that two simple measurements will always tell me their real place in a ministry's pecking order: (1) the percentage of adults who attend a small group, and (2) the participation level of senior staff and key lay leaders.

Critical Mass

By far the most important of these measures is the participation level of a church's leaders. If they're fully and visibly involved, the congregation usually follows. It's the key to reaching critical mass—the all-important stage at which the full power and benefits of a small group ministry begin to impact the ethos, DNA, and spiritual health of nearly everything and everyone.

Getting there usually requires that somewhere between 40 to 60 percent of the average weekend adult attendance be involved in a small group. If fewer people participate, small groups will still have a profound effect, but it will be primarily on the individuals in them, not on the entire church.

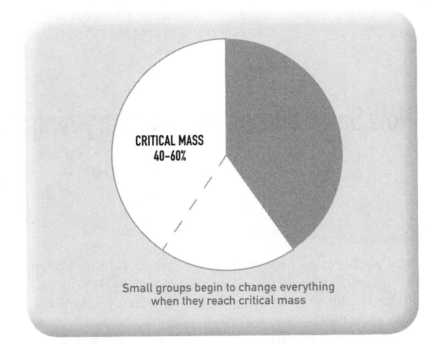

CRITICAL MASS 40–60%

Small groups begin to change everything
when they reach critical mass

That's not to say small groups aren't worth the effort if you can't reach critical mass right away — or ever. They'll still have great value in the lives of those involved. But their impact will never equal the revolutionary results that occur when small groups reach the level of a core ministry, or better yet the hub around which a ministry revolves.

At North Coast Church, small groups have been the hub for decades. But it wasn't always so. In the beginning they weren't even an important part of our ministry. For the first five years, the few small groups we had were decidedly peripheral. I wasn't involved, and neither were any of our elders.

However, once we took the steps necessary to make them a genuine priority — by hiring a staff member to wake up thinking about small groups and by clarifying the expectation that *all* leaders would participate — the impact on the health and spiritual DNA of our church was profound and nearly immediate.

In fact, I was shocked by how quickly the culture of the entire church began to change. It's a pattern I've since seen in church after church. It doesn't matter if the groups are sermon based or not. Ours weren't initially. All that matters is that a significant percentage of the congregation begins to meet in small gatherings outside the church building to share life and study the Bible together.

In the following section, we'll see what happens when that occurs.

The Holy Man Myth

One of the first things I noticed was the demise of a great falsehood that cripples our churches: the Holy Man myth.

It's the idea that pastors and clergy somehow have a more direct line to God. It cripples a church because it overburdens pastors and underutilizes the gifts and anointing of everyone else. It mistakenly equates leadership gifts with superior spirituality.

Here's how it impacted me. If someone in our church needed prayer, advice, or simply a visit in the hospital, I was the only one they wanted. If someone else showed up, apparently their prayers wouldn't take and their advice wouldn't work. And if I never made it to the hospital, the patient was sure to complain, "No one from the church ever visited me" — even though their friends (who were all from the church) stopped by daily.

I could never figure out how people's seeming dependence on my prayers, advice, and physical presence squared with our stated belief in the priesthood of the believer — the New Testament doctrine that every follower of Christ has the privilege of direct access to God. It's hardly a peripheral doctrine. It's one that God himself emphasized when he ripped open the temple curtain that had, until Jesus' death, separated the Holy of Holies from everyone but the high priest. This event symbolized the end of an era when a special holy man was needed to stand in the gap to mediate between God and man.[3]

Small groups undercut this Holy Man myth because they typically meet in widely dispersed settings. This makes it impossible for the pastor (or any other staff member) to carry out all the pastoral roles and functions. They simply can't be everywhere at once.

As a result, small group leaders inevitably step up and assume roles of spiritual leadership that they would have otherwise deferred to the pastoral staff.

That not only changes the way small group leaders view themselves; it changes the congregation's outlook as well. Once people begin to realize that God's anointing and spiritual power aren't restricted to the guy who speaks each Sunday, they whine a lot less when he's not available.

The Holy Place Myth

Another spiritually crippling falsehood that began to lose its grip on our congregation was what I call the Holy Place myth. It's the idea that God's presence is somehow greater in some places than in others.

It's why some Christians will tell a joke at the office they'd never think of repeating at church. It's why others don't think twice about lying on a loan application but still swear they live by the Ten Commandments.

The Holy Place myth fosters a false dichotomy between the secular and the spiritual by leading us to believe that there are some places where God hangs out and lots of others he seldom frequents.

A significant small group ministry undercuts this myth because when people begin to see God at work in their apartments and living rooms, they start to realize that a baptism can take place in a swimming pool, that Communion can be celebrated around a dining table, and that God is just as likely to answer their prayers in the front room as he is to answer mine in the front of the sanctuary.

With the demise of both the Holy Man and the Holy Place myths, our ministry was, for the first time, genuinely unleashed. People started bringing God to the workplace and into their neighborhoods rather than trying to bring everyone to the church building. And they quit insisting that I or another staff member had to show up in order for God to show up.

Once people start taking ministry into their own hands, they discover they're pretty good at it. So much so that if I ever tried to return to the old days of centering ministry around the Holy Man and the Holy Place, I'd have a mini-riot on my hands.

Once people get a taste of frontline ministry, they don't let it go easily. Once the church has been let loose, it's hard to put it back in the box.

Genuine Empowerment

Still another powerful advantage of a churchwide commitment to small groups is the number of opportunities it creates for significant ministry.

Let's face it: In most churches there aren't that many opportunities for high-impact, life-on-life ministry. There are usually a few up-front teaching roles, a handful of worship leader positions, and some youth and Sunday school slots to be filled. After that, most roles are pretty much part of the supporting cast, designed more to keep the machine running than to touch lives.

Small groups open up lots of new opportunities for frontline ministry. At North Coast every group has a leader and a host, most often made up of two couples. That means in every group, we have four people who teach, counsel, disciple, pray, visit hospitals, lead in worship, provide Communion, and even baptize members of their little flock—none of which they would do without the platform for ministry we call a growth group.

Empowerment without a platform is like responsibility without authority. In too many of our churches, we offer discipleship training and leadership training without providing any significant platform for people to do the things they've been trained to do.

This is especially true in our larger churches. While a big church needs lots of people to fill background and support roles, it doesn't necessarily need any more teachers, worship leaders, or other up-front people than a midsized or even a small church.

Worse, in some (though not all) megachurches, the span of ministry is so large that only the best of the best ever get a chance to exercise leadership and pastoral functions. But small groups alleviate this problem, because every group provides a platform for those who've been empowered and released to do the work of the ministry.

As a former youth pastor, I learned long ago that no one steps up *until* there's a vacuum that needs to be filled. Every year when my seniors were about to graduate, I would wonder if we'd survive without their leadership. But as soon as they were gone, the juniors and sophomores stepped up—often doing a better job than their departing upperclassmen.

I've found that this same principle applies churchwide. Having lots of positions that need to be filled is not a bad thing. It causes people who otherwise would sit back and observe to step forward and become leaders.

A platform for significant ministry not only allows people to do things they'd never do otherwise; it can also motivate them to strive to live up to the higher spiritual standard that usually goes with the role.

I remember playing golf with one of our new small group leaders. Off the tee, he hit a terrible shot. Then he said a terrible word.

As if on cue, he turned to me and said, "Whoops." And then he said something that I didn't expect. Instead of the usual "Sorry, Pastor, I forgot you were here," he said, "Man, I can't talk like that—I'm a growth group leader!"

I knew right then we'd turned a huge corner. Rather than being shamed by the presence of his pastor, he was shamed by his failure to live up to his new role in ministry. He saw this role as something that called him to a higher standard.

By the way, before you're too harsh on him, I have to tell you if you'd seen his slice, you'd understand.

Chapter 7

Still More Ways That Small Groups Change Everything

As we've already seen, a commitment to small groups will change your church. It releases people and unchains ministry. It empowers lay leaders by offering many more platforms for significant hands-on ministry.

But that's not all. A strong small group ministry can also help a church become more authentic in its relationships and far more disciplined in its spiritual disciplines. It can even break the cycle of young adults dropping out of church once they reach early adulthood and coming back once they get married and have kids.

In the next section, we'll see why and how.

Honesty and Transparency

Just stand around any Sunday and listen to the people in your church greet one another. You'll hear numerous varieties of "What's up? How you doing?"

But no matter how good or bad things are, you'll hear one predominant answer: "Fine!"

It doesn't matter if my marriage is falling apart, the kids broke curfew for the third night in a row, or I'm about to lose my job. The answer is always the same.

On one level it's understandable. Lots of times "How ya doing?" just means "I see you." We don't really want or expect an answer. But even when the question is sincere and the concern genuine, the answer is usually the same: "Fine. How about you?"

Now, there are a number of reasons why this is so. To begin with, in larger social settings, we're usually more concerned with image than honesty, especially when strangers or casual acquaintances might be listening in.

On top of that, the church doesn't exactly have the best record when it comes to responding to those who want to talk about struggles and hardship. We want everyone to be happy. We want to make God look good. We don't want to hang out our dirty linen in public. A non-Christian might hear and be turned off—or a gossip might hear and be turned on.

As a result, transparency is hardly the hallmark of most churches. So much so that for most people, the stereotype of a church is a place with lots of plastic smiles.

Small groups can change that, because by their nature and structure, they naturally foster greater honesty and transparency. Their location, size, and makeup are much more conducive to authenticity than any sanctuary or Sunday school class can ever hope to be.

Just think about it. Where would *you* be more likely to be open and honest?

In a living room or a classroom?

With twelve people or twenty-five people?

In a group where there's always a new face, or a group where you already know everyone?

For most of us, the answers would be the living room, the group of twelve, and the group where we know everyone. The small group setting wins hands down.

And over time, the honesty that naturally takes place in small groups begins to leak out into the entire church.

Fact is, most Christians don't know that it's okay to be honest, to share their problems, to ask for prayer for their own needs rather than Uncle Fred's battle with cancer. But once they learn it's okay to be real in their small group—that they won't be shot or ostracized—people tend to start being real in other places as well, eventually even at church.

I saw this quite clearly a number of years ago when we offered some small groups under the title "marriage renovation growth groups."

When I heard the name, I pulled the leaders together and informed them they'd have to change it because no one would sign up. It's just not the image most people want to project at church.

I suggested the name "marriage enrichment growth groups." But they resisted. They figured marriage enrichment groups would be too much like the local gym—full of people who didn't really need all that much help. They wanted people with stinking marriages.

So I told them okay, knowing they'd change the name the next week when no one signed up.

Instead the groups filled up the first weekend.

I was pumped. Not that we had so many marriages in trouble but that we had so many people willing to admit it. It was then I realized the impact our small groups had had on our church as a whole. After years of being honest in one another's homes, people thought nothing of being honest at church, even if it meant admitting that their marriages were all jacked up.

Spiritual Disciplines

Still another powerful advantage that small groups can bring is a marked increase in the practice of spiritual disciplines. That's because a small group takes our good intentions and puts them on our calendar.

Every church is full of people who feel they should do more when it comes to reading the Bible, prayer, fellowship, and reaching out to meet the needs of others. But busy schedules, procrastination, and a lack of commitment all conspire to keep these things from happening.

Small groups take these important but not particularly urgent spiritual disciplines and make them urgent by putting them on the schedule.

For instance, at North Coast we have an amazing prayer meeting that takes place virtually every week. Few people realize it's happening, because it is stealth, spread out throughout our community in different locations on different days.

But there are more people sharing intimate personal prayer requests and actually praying for one another than we could ever fit into our facility for a traditional prayer meeting.

Here's the irony: If we canceled our small groups and filled our facility once a week for a prayer meeting with standing-room-only crowds, we'd probably get some great write-ups in the Christian press. But in reality we'd have almost 70 percent fewer people praying than we already have in our weekly small groups.

Same with Bible study. Just the fact that group members have to prepare for the study and then go over it in their meeting causes lots of them to open a Bible that would otherwise be left on the nightstand.

The same goes for our service projects, fellowship, Communion, and a host of spiritual disciplines that our small groups move from the realm of "I should do it" to "I've done it" by simply putting them on the weekly schedule.

The Best Children's Program Ever

Even though our small groups are for adults only, we found that our children benefited greatly. In fact, the decision to make small groups the hub of our ministry resulted in our best and most effective children's program ever. Let me explain.

When I was a youth pastor, I noticed an all too familiar cycle. Little kids participated in a great children's program, moved on to a dynamic youth ministry, and graduated to a vibrant college program—then followed all this with a predictable postcollege or newlywed fadeout. That is, until they had their own kids to bring back to our wonderful children's and youth programs.

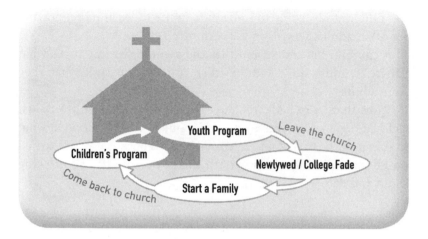

I wondered why we provided all kinds of Bible studies and spiritually stretching experiences for our children and youth but only sermons and Sunday school lectures for adults. I wondered why all the fun and discipleship ended at graduation, especially since most of the adults I knew still seemed to have some serious growing to do.

Around this time, I also began to wonder if the best gift we could give our children and youth might not be the great programs we were offering but instead be something different — the simple but profound gift of a growing mom and dad.

After all, it's a well-known fact that young adults tend to mimic the behavior patterns of their parents once they start to have their own families (despite all their protestations to the contrary while growing up).

I was always amazed at how much like their parents most of the kids in my youth group eventually became. Once they hit adulthood, our influence waned and their parents' influence held sway. They parented like they were parented, did marriage like their parents, and even did adult Christianity like it was modeled by most of the adults around them.

All this made me ask, What would happen if the children in our church saw their parents regularly opening their Bibles to prepare for a Bible study, going to someone's home to learn more, praying for other adults, serving in the community?

I came to the conclusion that they would assume that's what Christian adults do—and they'd start doing the same when they were adults.

Now that we've had enough years to follow the results, it's just as I had hoped. Our young adult dropout rate is a fraction of what I've seen in the past. And I'm convinced it's because we've focused on giving our children and youth the powerful gift of a growing mom and dad.

Chapter 8

Making the Message Memorable
How Sermon-Based Small Groups Made Me a Much Better Preacher

Like most pastors, I know that if I want my preaching to be powerful, it has to be memorable. That sounds simple enough— until you try to pull it off week in and week out.

Early in my ministry, I would spend hours putting a sermon together, hoping to change lives with biblical principles and insights, only to find out later that the only thing anyone remembered was the funny story about my kids or the illustration about getting lost in Seattle.

Communication experts told me the key to more memorable sermons was using more props and compelling stories. Other people told me to get rid of the gimmicks and stick to the meat of the Word. Some warned me to shorten my messages in light of shrinking attention spans. Still others pointed out that most of the best-known and most-listened-to pastors were seldom brief in their remarks. It was all a bit confusing.

Over the years, I've tried all kinds of things to drive home a point and make it stick—from shorter sermons to lengthy discourses, from narratives to hyperpractical five-step-program instructions, from verse-by-verse expositions to hot-button topics.

At one point we even hit the pause button in the middle of my sermons to allow for questions and discussion (something the extroverts loved and the introverts loathed).

Some things helped. Most didn't. Some were pretty ridiculous. But one thing did make a huge difference. It was something we stumbled upon a couple of years into our small group journey: *building our home studies around a discussion of the previous weekend's sermon.*

The decision to combine the sermon and our midweek small groups into a lecture-lab combo was at first a little risky. We'd always offered choices. Tying everything to the weekend message meant we were bucking our own tradition and the conventional wisdom that people want more, not fewer, choices.

To some of our folks, especially those who'd thrived in a free market of self-selected topics and book studies, asking everyone to use the same sermon-based curriculum (and writing it ourselves) felt like we'd suddenly gone high-control.

We went for it anyway, because we liked the potential upside. We thought it might offer significant educational benefits to study one thing and study it well rather than studying lots of things, none of which we ever covered in depth.

But one thing I didn't expect was that it would also make me a better preacher—maybe not a better one in the eyes of a preaching professor or homiletics expert, but a far better one in terms of my messages being memorable and life-changing. In the next section, we'll see why.

Increased Attentiveness

One of the first things I noticed was that people were more attentive.

I wish I could take credit for an improved delivery or better material, but I didn't really change anything. What changed was the congregation's awareness that they were going to discuss the message later. People who would normally fold their arms and listen paid careful attention—most even started taking notes. Those who missed a point were likely to catch me afterward to fill in what they missed.

I also discovered that attentiveness is contagious. When everyone else in the room is dialed in, it sends a subtle, maybe even subliminal, message that this is important stuff—don't miss it. So most people work a little harder to hang in there even during the slow (should I say boring?) parts of the message.

Increased Note Taking

The most obvious sign of greater attentiveness was the marked increase in note taking. That alone had a significant impact.

Educational theorists have long pointed out that we forget most of what we hear unless we also interact with the material visually, verbally, or physically. That's why getting people to take notes increases recall dramatically.

In every crowd there are always a good number of neurotic note takers (you know the type; they're the folks who get a nervous twitch if a blank in the sermon outline is left unfilled or a point is skipped over). The challenge is to get everyone else to also write something down.

That's not too hard to do when their small group questions are tied to the weekend message. Then even the most note-resistant listeners tend to write something down, because they know they'll be discussing the key points later in the week. Note taking is their way of "laying down some crumbs" so they can find their way back home again when their group meets.

Spirited Discussion

When I first entered the ministry, I dreamed of communicating God's Word so powerfully that people would mull it over and discuss it during the week. I envisioned impassioned discussions of the deep theological truth I'd presented in the sermon.

I must have been smoking something.

If truth be known, for most of our congregation the frantic pace of a typical week quickly pushed Sunday's sermon to the background. The thought of sitting down and carefully reviewing what they'd heard at church never entered their mind. They were too busy.

Shoot, so was I!

But once we started tying our small group questions to the weekend message, everything changed. Nearly everyone took time to review their notes and think back over the message. And even if they rushed through the homework a half hour before the meeting or on the way to the meeting with a flashlight in their mouth, telling their spouse, "Slow down, honey," I was still far ahead.

The stuff we'd talked about on Sunday morning was no longer buried in the recesses of their minds. For a few short hours it was once again front and center.

Better yet, they not only reviewed it; they also discussed it, and often with something close to the level of spirited dialogue I'd always dreamed of igniting.

Churchwide Focus

Sermon-based small groups also made it much easier for our teaching team to keep the entire church focused and headed in the same direction. Whether we're casting vision, clarifying direction, or simply dealing with an important issue, it's much easier to get people on the same page and keep them there.

I grew up in a church where we studied one passage or topic in the Sunday sermon, another in Sunday school, still another on Sunday night, and something entirely different on Wednesday night.

Frankly, I never had much of a clue as to what we were studying—something related to the Bible, I suppose. The teaching was far too disjointed to create any sense of focus, and for most of us it was more of a data overload than anything else.

Sermon-based small groups keep this from happening because they take one topic and ask the entire congregation to slow down and digest it together. By definition, they put everyone on the same page—and make them look at that page more than once. The result is always a greater sense of common direction and reference. And our groups make whatever we're teaching far more memorable.

Reaching More People

The switch to sermon-based small groups also allowed me to reach more people. That's because those who miss church or serve in some area of our ministry are much more likely to get a CD or download the sermon if they're in a sermon-based small group.

I'd like to think our teaching team's messages are so amazing that no one wants to miss out. But the truth is that we have a huge spike in CD orders and downloaded sermons when our sermon-based small groups are in session. We also know that most of these are listened to by more than one person—the congregation member and a spouse, a roommate, or a friend.

That means hundreds of people who otherwise wouldn't hear the message not only hear it but reflect on it and then go to a small group to discuss it. That ought to bring joy to any preacher's heart.

Beyond Familiarity

Still another way in which our sermon-based small groups make me a better preacher can be found in how they help me move people beyond mere exposure to actual knowledge.

One reason I want my messages to be memorable is that I want people to apply the important spiritual truths and doctrines of the faith. I know that if I can change the way people think, it will change the way they live.

But every time I teach, I have a significant roadblock to overcome. It's our natural tendency to confuse familiarity with knowledge.

Basically, there are four stages of knowledge. The first is what I call the *inspired* stage. That's what happens when I hear a new truth or principle that rings true. I'm inspired and challenged. I go home thinking, "Boy, I learned something today."

The second stage is *familiarity*. It's the stage at which I hear something and go, "Oh yeah, I remember that." It's not particularly exciting, but if it fits with where I'm living and the issues I'm

INSPIRED ➡ FAMILIARITY ➡ BORED ➡ KNOWLEDGABLE

We don't always know what we think we know

facing, it can be challenging and send me home with the feeling, "I'm glad I came."

The third stage is the *bored* stage. It's when I've heard it all before and feel like there's nothing more to learn. It's the stage that most communicators dread and try to avoid as much as possible. But it's not yet real knowledge—it's only deep familiarity. And it's the stage at which many of us bail out.

I've only reached the *knowledge* stage when I know the principle or truth *before* someone brings it up and reminds me, when I can state it or use it without being prompted.

I often have people come up to me after a sermon and show me their outline, pointing out some blanks they filled out before the message began. You can see in their eyes and sly smile a sense of "Look, I got you!"

In reality I got them. If they're jotting down a passage, a point, or one of my favorite sound bites before I say it, they've come to the point of knowing the information. In the ultimate sense, my message has become memorable.

But here's the problem: Because we hate so badly to bore people, most teachers don't repeat anything often enough to move beyond

Sermon-based small groups help make the message memorable through multiple inputs

the deep familiarity of boredom to the point of true knowledge. And that leaves our people with lots of things they *kinda know.*

One of the great advantages of a sermon-based lecture-lab model is that it exposes people multiple times to a passage, principle, or spiritual truth. It helps move them from the inspired and familiarity stages toward a working knowledge of God's Word and biblical principles.

And it happens simply because the process makes everyone listen more attentively, encourages note taking, causes most people to review the sermon once again, and then ends in a spirited discussion with friends.

That's a process that would make anything more memorable— even *my* preaching.

If you ever want to help people understand the difference between familiarity and knowledge, just ask ten or twenty people if they think it's important to live by the Ten Commandments.

After they say yes, tell them you can't remember all the commandments and ask them to help you list them.

You'll find that most can't. They believe in these laws and try to follow them. They just don't know what they are or how to find them!

You can do the same thing with many other "well-known" biblical passages and concepts. You'll discover lots of familiarity but not so much knowledge.

By the way, you can find the Ten Commandments listed in Exodus 20:1 – 17. Not that *you* needed to know. But your friend might read this book.

Chapter 9

Making the Message Accessible
How Sermon-Based Small Groups Made Us a Much Better Church

Sermon-based small groups not only made me a better preacher; they made us a better church. That's because the lecture-lab model makes the Scriptures far more accessible, and the task of leading a small group much more manageable. The model even makes it easier to find and train leaders.

On good days it can turn straw into gold and water into wine.

Okay, maybe not. But the sermon-based model has provided our church with so many benefits that I can't imagine ever going back. Let's take a look at just a few more of them.

Reeling in the Marginally Interested

Like every church, we have our share of spiritual window-shoppers and casual Christians. To my thinking, that's a good thing. They're exactly the people who need Jesus most.

They're easy to recognize. They sit through the sermon with a glazed look, their minds obviously dialed in on something else. They never open a Bible. They don't even bring one. If a story is really good or funny, they'll check in for a moment or two—but then check out again long before the spiritual application. I've also noticed that they look at their watches a lot—even during the first few minutes.

They're a preacher's nightmare. Sometimes they seem unreachable. Often they are.

But our sermon-based small groups have proven to be a powerful tool for reeling them in. That's because the moment they sign up (even if it's just to appease a spouse or hang out with some friends), we've got them on the hook. Immediately their connection with the worship service and sermon changes, and when that changes, so does everything about their church experience.

Let's take Marginal Mark as an example. He comes to church primarily for his wife and kids. During a typical sermon, he day-dreams about his job, some major decisions he's facing, or his fantasy football team. He's a moral guy, just not too "religious." He'd rather leave the extra stuff for those who are really into it.

Now let's imagine that his wife gets him to sign up for a sermon-based small group. Suddenly, despite his previous lack of interest, he's listening at a deeper level. He'll almost certainly start taking some notes. Then he'll look at them again, however briefly, before the meeting. At the meeting, with some friends in a safe and non-judgmental environment, he'll discuss the Scriptures and what it means to follow Jesus.

The hook has been set.

He's now interacting with the Word of God at a level far beyond anything he's ever done before. And in most cases it won't be long until the Scriptures start to do their stuff — convicting him, instructing him, and training him in a righteousness he didn't even know he was looking for.

This is often the first time a guy like Marginal Mark gets close enough to the Bible to even know what it says, much less to realize how alive and practical it can be. And for a guy like him, that's often the biggest hurdle to clear before making a full commitment to follow Jesus instead of just going to church.

It's a story I've seen played out time after time. A spouse or friend joins a group to keep the peace or just to check it out. But once they start interacting with Scripture and it begins to sink in, they move from marginal to enthusiastic — ofttimes even becoming a host or leader of their own group.

It's an exciting process to watch. What makes it all the better is that it's all so organic. It doesn't take a lot of monitoring, pushing, or cajoling. In fact, that would probably short-circuit the process. It just takes stepping back and letting the powerful mixture of God's Spirit, his people, and the Scriptures do its work.

As natural as this process is in a sermon-based group, it's not so easy to pull off in a more traditional small group structure.

To begin with, without a natural connection to what goes on in the weekend service, it's harder to get Marginal Mark to even try a group. It's a relatively short step from listening to a sermon to joining a small group that discusses the sermon he's already heard. But it's a much bigger step into a traditional small group Bible study. That's because if people don't perceive a natural connection to the worship service, they tend to feel like they're signing up for the equivalent of a spiritual honors course — hardly the type of thing most window-shoppers or marginally interested Christians are looking for.

And even if Marginal Mark does join a group and begins to grow, the isolated nature of the study material gives him no reason or motivation to connect with the larger body of Christ, the worship service, or the weekend message. Odds are, he'll still sit through it as bored and disinterested as ever.

Mainstreaming New Christians

Sermon-based groups also make it easier to mainstream new believers. That's because these groups tend to be less intimidating for those who lack any spiritual or biblical background.

A hypothetical scenario shows why.

I'm not into movies. It's not a spiritual thing; they just usually bore me. Now, suppose I found myself in a theater arts class at the local community college. Most likely, I'd be the only one who didn't know much about movies. You can bet that most of the time, I wouldn't say much. I'd be too intimidated, fearful of looking stupid or exposing my ignorance.

But if the discussion turned to one of the few movies I've paid money to see, that's different. I'm in. I'm all in.

That's because, like most people, I consider myself to be an expert on whatever I've personally experienced. I don't care if everyone else hated it or loved it; I have my own opinion and I'll make it known.

Yet the moment the class reverts back to a discussion of movies in general, I'm back on the sidelines, no longer so sure of the value or accuracy of my viewpoints.

That's exactly how most new Christians feel when they join a study group. If it's a generic discussion of a biblical passage or workbook, they won't say much.

But if it's a discussion about a sermon they've heard and experienced, most of them will be much quicker to share their thoughts and insights. Especially if the questions are phrased in a way that asks, "What did you think of ...?" "How do you feel when ...?" "What jumped out at you most and why?"

These types of questions can't really have a wrong answer. Not when they are applied to something that everyone feels like they experienced more than studied.

All this has made it relatively easy for us to mainstream new Christians, putting them in whatever group has an opening.

In some churches, a concern over the intimidation that new and not-yet Christians can feel in the presence of Bible-quoting, flip-to-the-passage Christians has led to a pattern of separating them from longtime Christians. In fact, I've often heard it passed off as conventional wisdom that longtime Christians can kill a study for window-shoppers and new Christians, so they should be kept as far away as possible.

While I understand the desire to remove the intimidation factor, something seems wrong with a world where we remove all the adults from the nursery.

The truth is, if we want to disciple people, the best thing to do is not to separate out all the newbies. It's to get them into a situation where they can rub shoulders with longtime Christians and benefit from life-on-life modeling and mentoring from those who've learned what it means to live out their faith on a day-to-day basis.

Better Prepared

There's still another advantage that comes with a lecture-lab small group model. It's that most people (including the marginally interested and new Christians) come to the meeting far more prepared than they would if they were using a typical workbook or study guide.

It's no secret that lots of homework questions are answered right before the meeting—maybe on the way to the meeting. That can lead to shallow answers and shallower discussions.

But the lecture-lab structure of a sermon-based small group makes a large part of the preparation almost effortless. Because they've already heard the sermon, everyone comes to the meeting with at least forty-five minutes of preparation (the length of a typical weekend sermon at North Coast). Add to that the time spent on homework, even if it's rushed through at the last minute, and you have a significant amount of pre-meeting prep.

Frankly, I don't know how many window-shoppers, marginally interested people, or new Christians would faithfully spend forty-five minutes filling out a study guide or even watching an assigned video. But in our setting, small group members invest that much time in preparation before every meeting. Even those who miss the sermon find a way to listen online or swing by the church to pick up a CD. And that means people come to the group far more prepared for discussion than they would have been under most any other method or model.

Ironically, if we told the window-shoppers, the marginally interested, or the new Christians that they'd have to spend nearly an hour preparing for each meeting, few if any of them would ever sign up. So we don't tell them. We just let them start out without ever pointing out what they're doing.

Finding Leaders

It's also much easier to find leaders in a sermon-based model. That's because it takes a less experienced and less knowledgeable leader to lead a discussion than it does to lead an inductive Bible study or guide a group through a workbook.

Effectively leading a traditional small group Bible study usually requires a good deal of biblical knowledge, at least some degree of a teaching gift, and a significant amount of pre-meeting preparation.

And that leaves a lot of people out.

The high standard of leadership needed to maintain a quality experience for everyone is one of the reasons why so many traditional small groups disband and why it's hard to keep leaders over the long haul.

In contrast, sermon-based small groups only need a facilitator who has a growing relationship with God and a heart for the people in the group. These kinds of people are pretty easy to find, much easier than teachers with lots of Bible knowledge and extra time on their hands.

Frankly, if we were using traditional workbooks and study guides, we'd have far fewer groups and a much lower retention rate for both leaders and participants.

No More Idiot Questions!

Finally, one of the most annoying things about being in a small group is what I call the idiot questions. It seems as if every workbook and study guide has plenty of them. They're the questions with blindingly obvious answers.

I used to think, "Come on, can't we skip this stuff?"

But in reality we can't. The idiot questions are a necessary part of the process. They make sure everyone is on the same page and understands the background and context of the more substantive things we'll talk about later. There's really no way around them.

However, in a sermon-based small group, these context-setting questions are largely unnecessary, because the sermon establishes the context and framework for the study. As our staff likes to remind our teaching team, "The idiots up front have already answered all those questions for us."

Part 3

SERMON-BASED

SMALL

GROUPS

Chapter 10

Why Some Groups Jell and Some Don't

When people hear that for over twenty-five years, we've had 80 percent of our average weekend adult attendance meeting in sermon-based small groups, the questions come like a flood:

- How do you get such a high percentage?
- How do you find enough leaders?
- How do you train and keep them?
- What does a typical meeting look like?
- Who writes the questions?
- What about childcare?
- How do you put people into groups?

And so on.

The rest of this book will attempt to answer these questions and more as we explore the nuts and bolts of sermon-based small groups and their power to naturally close the back door. Though this model can now be found in a wide cross section of churches, most of what follows has been drawn from my experience at North Coast Church, where these groups have kept our back door tightly shut for decades—from our earliest days as a small church to the multiple thousands we serve today.

Before diving into the details and overarching principles, there is one thing I must emphasize. The secret sauce isn't found in our specific format, procedures, or administrative structures.

It's found in the process.

Anytime a group of friends commit to gather together to share their lives, pray, and discuss the biblical text and life application of the previous weekend's sermon, good stuff happens. In fact, the first time I ever experienced the power of such a group, it started spontaneously, without any guidelines or formal structure. We were just a few friends who wanted to help each other grow. Yet it had as great an impact as any group I've ever been in.

At North Coast, all we've done is find ways to institutionalize this simple process in order to motivate and involve as many people as possible. While my friends and I were able to pull it off on our own, we weren't able to sustain it over the long haul. If we'd known what follows, we might have been. Certainly, some of the things I advocate won't fit or work in your unique ministry context. That's okay. Toss them aside and grab hold of the principles and practices that will work. Use them as a starting point for developing your own model of sermon-based small groups.

With that said, let's take a look under the hood.

The Right Size

When it comes to small groups, size matters. If a group is too small, it has a hard time surviving. If it's too large, it has a tough time remaining sticky. Over the years, we've discovered that the ideal size for a sermon-based small group depends on a number of variables.

One has to do with comfort zones. A group needs to be small enough that everyone has a chance to contribute, but large enough that no one feels forced to speak up or share more than they want to. That means the ideal size for a group of introverts will tend to be larger than the ideal size for a group of think-it-and-immediately-say-it extroverts. One needs more people to break the silence. The other needs less people so that there will be some silence.

Another important factor is marital status. The ideal size for a group of married couples is usually twelve to fourteen people. For singles, eight to twelve can be ideal. That's because a group of six couples has a radically different dynamic than one with a dozen singles. Most married couples have a me-too partner, someone who almost always agrees with whatever their mate says (at least in public). While there are certainly plenty of exceptions, this pattern has proven to be so prevalent that when it comes to small groups, I've learned to think of married couples as one unit instead of two individuals.

The upshot is that while a group of six to eight singles can work quite well, a group with only three or four couples is usually too small to sustain long-term energy and focus. If one spouse is sick or absent, the other tends to stay home. In a group of eight people, that leaves the host and leaders with only one other couple besides themselves. It's an awkward dynamic that lends itself more to just hanging out than diligently working through the assignment.

On the flip side, when a group gets too large, it loses stickiness. We've found that whenever a couples group reaches sixteen people (or a singles group reaches fourteen), attendance becomes predictably inconsistent. It's strange, but we can have three groups of twelve people, and all thirty-six will be present at almost every meeting. But two groups of sixteen people will hardly ever have all thirty-two show up. Perhaps it has to with those in the smaller group feeling more needed and feeling a greater sense of responsibility. I'm not sure. But whatever the cause, it's a pattern that has held true for years.

That doesn't mean we forbid groups from reaching sixteen. We don't want to be that high-control. If a leader thinks he or she can break through the barrier, we warn them and then step back and let them try. But we already know what they'll soon learn. When a group gets too large for everyone to contribute or for those who don't show up to be missed, stickiness goes out the window.

The Right People

Even if a group is right-sized, if it has the wrong people, it won't stay together long.

Idealists always tell me that any group of Christians ought to be able to jell simply because of their shared unity in Christ. But anyone who gets out of the ivory tower long enough to see how life actually works will realize that there is a great difference between our spiritual unity in Christ and the special bond that comes with a deep friendship.

Unity in Christ means loving one another with an *agape* love that overcomes our differences. It's not uniformity; it's not finding the lowest common denominator. It's love despite our diversity. In fact, our unity in Christ shines brightest when we disagree most. It's Simon the Zealot rooming with Matthew the tax collector. It's Gentile Christians in Corinth collecting money to help the destitute Jewish Christians in Jerusalem. It's James and the Jerusalem council writing a letter of recommendation for Paul and his ministry to Gentiles.

Deep friendships are different. They're built on strong commonality. While it's true that close friends often have significant differences, they always have a stronger set of shared interests, values, or experiences that binds them together.

Jesus himself had differing layers of friendship. Out of all his disciples, he handpicked twelve apostles. Out of the apostles, he was particularly close to three (John, James, and Peter). And at least according to John, he had one he was closer to than all the rest. The one John's gospel cryptically calls "the disciple whom Jesus loved." None other than John himself!

How's that for humility?

We've found that the sermon-based small groups that have the greatest life-on-life impact and stay together the longest are always those in which the friendships are deepest. That's why we tell people to choose a group primarily according to who else is in it rather than where or when it meets.

Assigning people to groups by neighborhood sounds great on paper, but it seldom works well in real life (with the exception of new neighborhoods in an expanding community or in a wealthy town with lots of gated communities). That's because one of the poorest predictors of a potential deep friendship is the neighborhood we live in. In most cases, it doesn't indicate anything other than shared economic status. A much stronger likelihood of future friendship exists when we build groups around shared interests or a common station in life.

That's why we've instituted groups for singles, peace officers, newlyweds, blended families, parents of teens, and a host of others. I call the people in these groups "schooling fish" because they naturally stick together and easily accept and bond with others who share their same interests or station in life. Although we allow people to pick any group they want as long as there's room in the group, we've found that those who make their choice based on a convenient location or time have a much lower stick rate than those who look for a group with which they already share an interest or station in life.

Every year we have some folks who idealistically want to be in a group of all ages and stages. So they seek out one with multiple generations, blue-collar workers and business owners, Republicans and Democrats. After the first couple of meetings, they always tell me how great it is. By the end of the next quarter, they've usually signed up for a new group.

There is one grouping that works particularly well. It's what we call New Groups for New People. In this case, the strong similarity among the group members is not so much a shared interest or station in life as it is a shared lack of established relationships.

I think of people as being like Legos. We all have a limited number of connectors. Introverts have a few. Some extroverts have dozens. But either way, once they're full, they're full. And when that happens, we tend to be friendly but to not connect. It's what happens when you move to a new town and are excited by everyone's friendliness, only to be discouraged three months later that you haven't connected with anyone.

I'm an extrovert. I have lots of connectors. But due to my role and years in the community, I also have so many relationships that I don't have any empty connectors left. In fact, sometimes when my friends aren't looking, I'll take one of them off so I can connect with someone else for a while.

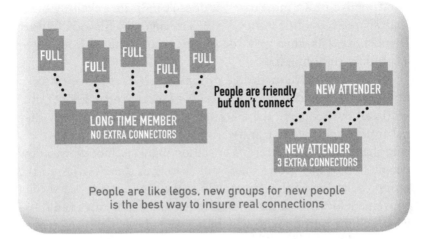

FULL FULL FULL FULL FULL

LONG TIME MEMBER
NO EXTRA CONNECTORS

People are friendly
but don't connect

NEW ATTENDER

NEW ATTENDER
3 EXTRA CONNECTORS

People are like legos, new groups for new people
is the best way to insure real connections

When Nancy and I meet someone new, we're very friendly. Say you've just moved into our neighborhood. We might bring you some fresh-baked cookies, invite you over for coffee or a barbeque. But to be honest, we won't connect on any sort of deeper level. If we have some extra time, tickets to a ball game, or a chance to have some friends over, we'll use it as an opportunity to reconnect with the people we're supposed to be close to but haven't seen in three weeks — or three months.

This can be very confusing and frustrating for people who are new to a community or church. The acts of friendship send one message, but the lack of connection sends another. It's why so many people complain about churches being cliquish.

The reality is, it's not so much a church full of cliques as it is a church full of people whose connectors are already full.

Obviously, this can be a huge problem when it comes to assimilating new people into a small group or even a congregation. But it can also be put to use by employing a bit of spiritual jujitsu.

New people, by definition, have lots of empty connectors. They usually share with other new people a very strong desire to get connected. This shared interest in developing new friends can become the foundation for close friendships that would otherwise be unlikely. You'll see this happening in any newly built neighborhood. Families move in with lots of empty connectors. As they put in a lawn, build a fence, or meet in the driveway, they connect and build relationships with much greater ease than they would have as a single family moving into an already existing neighborhood.

The result is often a tightly knit neighborhood made up of an eclectic group of people who otherwise might have had only a nodding acquaintance. The same holds true for our new groups for new people. The people in them tend to bond quickly. From a distance, these groups appear to be far less homogeneous than a typical station-in-life group. But in reality they are very homogeneous. All the members share a lack of existing relationships and a deep desire for connectedness. It's a strong bond on which to build.

Contrast this with the common practice of dividing existing groups to make more openings. The unintended consequence is often a case of friendliness without connection.

Those who come from the previously existing groups show up with an already overloaded set of connectors. While they might genuinely desire to reach out and build new relationships with those who are new to the group, their relational overload makes it unlikely that they will connect outside of the meeting. They don't have the time or the energy.

On the other hand, the new folks have lots of empty connectors. And while they are likely to appreciate the friendly atmosphere during the meeting, they're usually looking for something more than a couple of hours of friendly banter at a Bible study.

Chapter 11

Flies on the Wall

What Happens When a Sermon-Based Small Group Meets

For years, we've trained other churches and helped them launch their own version of sermon-based small groups. We've done it through both large conferences and customized workshops that we limit to just a couple of churches at a time. By far the most fun for me comes in the workshops: a two-day deep dive into the concepts and principles of sermon-based small group ministry.

Because the smaller size of these workshops allows all the participants to visit one of our small groups the evening after our first day of training, without fail the next day's training jumps to a new level. People come back with stories of groups that were awesome and some that were not so great. They tell of leaders diligently working their way through every question—in exact order—and others who never got past the first question. The workshop participants are always surprised that almost everyone showed up at the small group meeting with their homework filled out. And the participants usually comment on finding an even stronger sense of community and family than they expected.

But there is one other thing that inevitably comes up after comparing notes. People are blown away by how different all of the groups are from one another.

That's because in reality there is no such thing as a typical meeting in the sermon-based small group format. Each group and every session takes on its own flavor, based on the people in the group and the things happening in their lives. There is a basic template. But the model morphs into endless iterations so easily that our template functions more like a launching point than a blueprint. So it's with some hesitation that I write about what happens in a "typical" sermon-based small group.

Yet I know that if I don't, you're likely to read into the following pages definitions and assumptions that are based more on your own past experiences with small groups than what I'm trying to describe. It's the age-old problem of differing points of reference. We can use the same words, but different dictionaries. And it's why that firsthand visit by those in our customized workshops is always so valuable.

But since it's not possible to have every one of you reading this book visit one of our groups, I'll do my best to paint a picture of what you'd see and hear if you could be a fly on the wall at a sermon-based small group meeting here at North Coast Church.

In truth, this picture is more likely to look like what you'd experience in a new group or a group with a new leader, since we're pretty strict about insisting that our small groups follow the basic template in the beginning. This ensures that they get off to a good start. But after they've painted by numbers and done it exactly our way for a while, they usually begin to make some subtle changes to become the group that God is calling them to be.

Refreshments

In almost every case, the first thing you'd notice at one of our small group meetings is that it starts with some light refreshments as people arrive — especially something to drink.

That's because we want everyone to connect with some small talk and catch up from the previous week before sitting down and digging into the Scriptures. Extroverts might not need this time to power down or gear up, but most introverts do. And the extroverts don't mind. They love socializing anyway.

I'm sure you've noticed that everyone at a cocktail party walks around with a drink and something to munch on. It's not ravenous hunger or the desire for a buzz that causes them to do so. It's the social comfort that comes with having something in hand and something to do during the "slow" moments.

We find that these ten to fifteen minutes *before* the meeting are often some of the most important minutes of the meeting—not in terms of content but in terms of setting the tone for what happens next.

Sharing

Once the meeting starts, most groups spend fifteen to thirty minutes sharing prayer requests and updating one another on what has been going on in their lives.

This portion of the meeting usually takes on the personality of the people involved. Some groups are pretty formal with the process; others go with the flow. Some have to be cut off. Some are done in ten minutes. We don't insist that everyone shares. That would scare some folks away. And we train our leaders not to let anyone dominate. That would drive everyone else away.

As a group jells, this part of the meeting tends to expand and move to a much deeper level. In new groups, it can be perfunctory and shallow at first. But that's fine by us. We don't try to force depth. We simply provide an opportunity for great depth and vulnerability to show up when both the group and the Holy Spirit are ready.

Study and Discussion

The next part of the meeting is dedicated to the study and discussion of the previous weekend's sermon. It's designed to last somewhere around forty-five minutes.

To improve the quality of the discussion, we work hard to make sure that everyone comes with their answers to the study questions already filled out. One of the most effective ways we do this is by having our leaders periodically ask people to read what they've written down, especially if it appears that someone is deviating from their original answer.

It follows the old adage "Inspect what you expect." If a leader doesn't stay on top of this issue, it's not long until people show up without having even looked at the questions ahead of time, much less having written down an answer. And that's guaranteed to cut the breadth of the study and turn the study into a platform for those who like to think out loud.

We don't want anyone to be forced to think on their feet. So all the questions are provided in the worship bulletin beforehand (and posted on our website for those who miss the service or listen online).

This has two huge advantages. First, it keeps extroverts and those who like to shoot from the hip from dominating the meeting. Second, it undercuts the natural tendency we all have to let the first person who speaks set the tone and framework for everyone else's answer.

You've probably had it happen to you. A teacher or leader asks a question, and the first person who answers takes it in a totally different direction than you have in mind. If you're like most of us, you simply shift gears and answer in a way that fits with or builds on whatever the first person said.

While that's an understandable response, it's an idea and discussion killer.

Our first question is usually open ended. It might ask, "What did you find most challenging, helpful, or troubling?" That opens the door for those who want to discuss something we failed to include in the homework. It also gives the opportunity for anyone who's upset or confused by a point to say so.

While that might threaten some pastors, I figure people are already going to talk about the things they disagree with. Why not give them a safe and appropriate place to do so? If they're wrong, the group will usually set them straight. If I'm wrong, it's a good thing to have it pointed out.

The apostle Paul praised the people in a town called Berea because they didn't blindly take in everything he said.[4] Unlike others, they questioned his teaching and searched the Scriptures for themselves to see if what he said was so. I figured if that didn't bother an apostle, who am I to complain or shut down discussion?

We also intentionally supply more questions than most groups can get through in the allotted time. And we strongly encourage leaders *not* to go through every question—especially in order. But I must admit, we've not had the greatest luck getting our engineers to go through the questions out of order, or our accountant types to leave something out. You might pray for them.

Three Kinds of Questions

The homework always consists of three types of questions: Getting to Know Me, Into the Bible, and Application. They are seldom labeled as such, and they don't necessarily follow that order. But ideally every question should fall into one of these categories.

Getting to Know Me

These questions offer a nonthreatening look into our past or current life situations. They're designed to help us get to know each other at a safe but accelerated pace.

In new groups or at the beginning of a quarter, the questions might have nothing to do with what we're studying. They might ask, "What was your favorite summertime activity in high school?" or "What's your favorite flavor of ice cream?"

While these questions seem silly and worthless to many people—I confess hating them myself—they play an important role. They often reveal things we would not otherwise know about one another. They greatly speed up the process of getting to know everyone's history and background in an innocuous but illuminating way.

For instance, when someone answers that their favorite vacation back in high school was going to the family château in France, and someone else says they never had enough money for a vacation, it fills in lots of blanks. The one who annually took off for the château might now be a stay-at-home mom. The one raised without enough money for a vacation might now be a high-powered business-woman. Without some history-giving questions, you might never know some truths about people's pasts. Yet it's important information if we want to go beyond first impressions and facades.

As a group and the quarter progresses, these getting-to-know-me questions begin to come right out of the biblical text. For instance, "Which of the many characters in the parable of the prodigal son do you identify with most?" or "Was turning the other cheek considered a sign of strength or weakness in the home you were raised in?"

Into the Bible

These questions take the group to biblical passages that are either complementary or parallel to the main text of the sermon but were not covered in the message.

This is what keeps a sermon-based small group from feeling like a mindless regurgitation of what the pastor already said on Sunday. It's what allows some groups to go deep and others to stay fresh. It's what keeps the "smart people" coming back for more.

When someone from another church tells me their sermon-based small groups have a hard time retaining people, one of the first things I ask to see is their study questions. More often than not I find they've failed to provide any significant biblical material besides what was already covered in the sermon. For anyone with much of a biblical background or even a quick intellect, that's a ticket to boredom.

The result is usually a lot of complaints about the studies being too easy, not deep enough, or superficial. But what most folks really mean is that there was nothing new. They're basically saying, "I heard it all on Sunday."

Application

The third kind of questions we use are application questions. These are designed to take the main point or points of the sermon and drive them home. They typically deal with attitudes or life-change issues.

For instance, we might ask, "Which of the four types of prayers that we looked at this weekend comes most naturally to you, and which one do you need to add to your repertoire?"

Or we might ask, "This weekend we explored David's refusal to seek his own revenge when ridiculed and cursed by Shimei. Is there anyone in your workplace, school, or neighborhood whom you need to quit worrying about and turn over to God?"[5]

Sometimes we'll present a case study and ask, "Based on the principles we saw this weekend, what would you do if ...?"

By the way, we don't feel the need to provide an application question for every point in the sermon. Sometimes the entire lesson might deal with only one of the subpoints or subtopics covered in the message. Our goal is not to neurotically review everything the pastor says; it's to connect people to one another and get them to dig deeper into the Scriptures.

We also don't feel the need for every session to include a mega life-change question. You know the type: "What one thing from this message jumps out at you as a word from the Lord?" or "What one life-changing step is God asking you to take in response to the things we saw this week?"

The truth is, most of our sermons and small group meetings are nothing more than another step in the journey. While some are life-changing, most aren't. They're simply part of the process. When we ask each time about what earth-shattering truth people learned or what life-changing commitment they made, we simply cause them to tune out or lie.

Prayer

The last thing we ask every group to do each time they meet is to end with a time of prayer.

In most groups, the prayer component takes about fifteen to thirty minutes. Though we don't require it, most groups split up the men and women for prayer. And once they break into their smaller groups, they usually share some more requests before praying.

We ask everyone to use sentence prayers (one person praying for just one item at a time). This shuts down the long-winded dominator and enables those who are new or more introverted to pray out loud much more easily. Of course, if someone doesn't want to pray, they don't have to.

After prayer, most groups gather for some dessert and some socializing before everyone heads home.

Freedom to Digress

We generally give group leaders a great deal of freedom to digress should a special situation arise. We've had groups spend the entire evening in prayer or focused on a crisis in the life of a member. Some have fixated on a particular question or issue and drilled down on it for the entire session.

Though we try to keep new groups from digging in so deep and fast that they scare off newer Christians, we do allow groups that have been together longer to take on their own flavor or added emphasis.

In some cases, that has meant doing extra reading and study, memorizing Scripture, taking on a significant service project, or providing missionary support.

I'm fine with that, as long as it's a natural and organic spiritual progression that the group embarks on as a whole. The reality is that over time, most groups will take on the passions and interests of the group leader or members.

Since the process of sharing, study, and prayer is more important than any specific content we might provide, I don't care all that much if a group deviates, as long as it's led of the Spirit or in response to the needs of the group. The goal of our template is simply to give each group a map of the area as the Lord takes them on their own unique spiritual journey.

Worship

You've probably noticed that I haven't said anything about worship. By that I mean singing, which has somehow come to be considered the primary means of worship in most of our churches. But I'll show some restraint and leave that discussion for another time and place.

We give groups the freedom to choose whether to have a worship element. Some do and some don't. Sometimes it's a significant part of their spiritual journey together. Other times it appears to be nothing more than an uncomfortable warm-up for the real meeting.

Bottom line: We have not found worshiping together to be an essential element for a spiritually healthy and dynamic group. It can be a great thing. It's just not an essential thing.

Service Projects and Socials

We ask every group to take on at least one service project a year (the ideal is two) and to have at least one social gathering per quarter.

To make sure that good intentions become reality, we monitor the service projects. We also provide lots of hand-holding in the form of contacts and options for groups to choose from. While a group is free to choose its own projects, most groups pick from our list of alternatives.

At the first meeting of the quarter, when everyone goes over their group covenant, we ask them to set dates for their social gatherings and determine a process for selecting a service project.

So there you have it. A fly-on-the-wall look at one of our "typical" sermon-based small group meetings.

Now that we've got that under our belt, we're ready to dig into the details and principles that make these groups so sticky and spiritually fruitful.

Chapter 12

Overcoming the Time Crunch

It's no news flash that lots of people are hyperbusy and overcommitted. Whether it's a spiritual problem or simply a fact of life in our modern-day global village, I'm not sure.

When I read Christian magazines or listen to Christian radio, I think that it's the result of poor planning, misplaced priorities, and the never-ending carnal pursuit of more.

But when I spend time with single parents, mothers of preschoolers, or anyone who's trying to make do with minimum-wage-job skills, it's hard to see their lack of discretionary time as a spiritual problem.

The same goes for my friends who are self-employed or hold significant roles of leadership in the corporate world or government. A union job might require only forty hours a week, but the world of small business and the executive suite demand fifty to sixty hours just to keep up, much less to get ahead.

To minister effectively in this fast-paced culture, programs and ministries have to take this epidemic of busyness into account. It does no good to ignore it, and even less good to rail against it. It's a reality we have to deal with.

Two Time Slots

As I travel across the nation, speaking to leaders from various denominational, theological, and socioeconomic backgrounds, I've found they all say the same thing. As a rule of thumb, most people will participate in only two time slots a week. No matter what that third meeting is for or when it takes place, it's hard to get anyone to show up.

Certainly, there are exceptions. Every church has some ministry animals who show up whenever the doors are open or there's an opportunity to serve. In addition, those who serve in key lay leadership positions often give more than a couple of time slots. But the pattern seems to hold true for most people. It's two time slots, with an occasional extra meeting or special event thrown in.

At North Coast we've chosen to adjust our ministry to this reality. Our entire church and our sermon-based small groups are designed to work within the two-time-slot paradigm.

It might not be the ideal, but it's what we have to work with. And since we believe so strongly that everyone (not just those with time on their hands) needs to have significant relationships to become spiritually healthy and mature, we've adapted our programs and ministry to fit within the time slots people will give us.

While some may see this as a spiritual compromise, I see it as following in the footsteps and spirit of the apostle Paul.[6] If I were a missionary in South America, I wouldn't insist on starting every worship service on time—even if I thought that being on time is an important sign of respect for God and a symbol of his priority in our life. Why? Because if I did, I'd be the only one there.

Same goes for designing a ministry that expects people to give more time than they are willing or able to give. I can do it. But nobody will show up.

Cutting the Competition

I find that most churches have far too many things on the docket. North Coast is no exception. Over time, we've added new programs and ministries to meet needs and seize opportunities. But once those programs are in place, it's hard to kill them off. Instead of giving a dead and dying program a nice Christian burial, we tend to put it on life support.

In a two-time-slot world, that can be a huge drain. It creates excessive competition for the limited time people do have to give.

To ensure that the most important and productive ministries thrive, it's necessary to periodically prune the programs and ministries that are least effective or most draining. In other words, we need to find ways to cut the competition as much as possible.

At North Coast that has meant a series of tough decisions (some rather unpopular at the time). We've had to say no to many great ideas and programs that would have broadened our ministry but blunted our impact.

For instance, from the beginning we decided not to provide adult Sunday school classes, choirs, special midweek children's programs, sports teams, midweek prayer meetings, additional Sunday night worship, and a host of other good but potentially competitive programs.

Now, I'm not trying to denigrate any of these ministries, nor am I advocating that a church that already has them get rid of them right away—or ever, for that matter. But I am saying that as long as they're in play, the percentage of people able and willing to be involved in a small group ministry will be significantly decreased.

We chose to radically cut competition because we felt that none of these other programs had the potential to provide the breadth and depth of significant relationships, or the laserlike focus on God's Word, that we could achieve with sermon-based small groups.

We also knew that if given the choice, many people would pick the ministry they enjoyed the most, not the ministry they needed the most.

At one point the only programming we offered was a Sunday morning worship service, children's and youth classes, and our small groups.

It often led to the following exchange.

"How can I get involved?"

"Try a growth group."

"I'm not much into small groups. What else do you have?"

"Well, we have Tuesday night growth groups."

"Anything else?"

"How about Wednesday night growth groups?"

We weren't too far off from Henry Ford's response in the early days of the Ford Motor Company. When people asked in what colors they could order their Model T, he reportedly told them they could have any color they wanted as long as it was black.

In our case, you could meet and connect with people any way you wanted, as long as it was in a growth group. Like Henry Ford, we discovered that while people might whine and complain about wanting more options, in the end, if it's all they can get, they'll drive away in whatever we have.

Without cutting the competition so severely, there is no way we ever could have reached an 80 percent participation rate in our small group program. And without keeping things trimmed back, we wouldn't have been able to sustain it, either.

Admittedly, it's much easier to cut the competition in a small or start-up ministry. All you have to do is say no.

In more-established ministries, layer upon layer of competition already exists. Churches with a strong history of adult Sunday school classes, midweek children's programs, choirs, or sports ministries have way too many champions and stakeholders to allow for such radical pruning. Cutting too deeply or too quickly won't reduce competition as much as it will stir up conflict.

When that's the case, it's best to simply stop adding new programs and let the dying ones die. Over time, this will create a void large enough for sermon-based small groups to thrive.

I have often reminded those who wish they could make a quicker transition to remember the lesson of the glacier and the avalanche. The glacier seems to be accomplishing nothing as it inches along. The avalanche makes a big ruckus. One creates a Yosemite. The other leaves hardly a trace a few years after it's gone.

Hamstring the Competition

While the competition can't always be cut, it can almost always be hamstrung.

As our church has grown larger and more complex, we've added plenty of new ministries and programs capable of sabotaging the participation levels in our sermon-based small groups. But to keep that from happening, we've learned to always ask, "How will this impact our growth groups?" And if we don't like the answer, we'll either delay the launch or tweak the program until we're satisfied the answer is, "Not much."

For instance, we have a ministry called North Coast U. It's a series of classes designed to teach basic theology, biblical content, and Christian life skills.

For years I resisted the pressure to add these so-called deeper classes. I felt there were already plenty of opportunities to get this material through parachurch ministries, publishing houses, and the Christian community at large.

I was also concerned that too many of our best leaders would prefer hanging out with other leaders ruminating on the deep things of theology, rather than jumping into the trenches to deal with the messy things of frontline ministry.

But after years of being asked, I finally said yes.

I still wasn't convinced. But enough of my key leadership was that it seemed foolish to dig in my heels. If there's wisdom in the counsel of many, it makes sense to listen and follow their advice from time to time.

But first I put two conditions on the classes. They had to be held in short, four-week blocks, and they could not begin or be promoted until after we'd started a new growth group quarter. This guaranteed that no one would sign up for a North Coast U class instead of a sermon-based small group.

No question. That significantly hamstrings North Coast U. But it doesn't kill it.

Yes, it undercuts its ability to be all that it could be. Less people participate. Teachers have a hard time figuring out how to teach theology or anything of significant complexity in four bite-sized snippets.

But it's kept our sermon-based small groups from being harmed by friendly fire. Those who really want or need the "deeper study" now have it available—at a price, the price of giving up a third time slot for four weeks in a row.

We've done something similar with virtually all our new ministries and programs. Before they launch and during any midcourse evaluations, the key question is always, "How is this impacting our sermon-based small groups?"

If we don't like the answer, we don't start the ministry. If it's already started, we hamstring it some more.

Leader Meetings

Another area where the time crunch inevitably rears its ugly head is in the recruitment and training of lay leaders. I've come to believe that one of the major reasons it's so hard to find and keep quality leaders in our churches is that we've chased them away with unrealistic time demands.

Many of our best church leaders are also leaders in the workplace or community. This is a good thing. It's part of being salt and light. It gets the salt out of the saltshaker. But I've also found that many pastors and staff members fail to grasp the time commitment this demands. They don't realize that their pet program or ministry isn't the only significant thing on the plate of their key lay leaders. So they plan way too many meetings that run way too long.

Back when one of the first waves of small group interest hit the American church, it came with a leadership training model that called for monthly leaders' meetings as well as extra coaching and mentoring.

It sounded great on paper. But in most cases it was like pulling teeth to get leaders to show up. What we intended as a reward for our leaders quickly became a measure of a leader's commitment and willingness to sacrifice for the good of the ministry.

I remember when we first started. We spent countless hours to prepare training of the highest caliber. In fact, many commented that it was better than anything they'd ever received in the business world. The food was great (and expensive). We provided an all-day fall kickoff, a monthly leaders' meeting, a halftime charge-'em-up, and a festive end-of-the-year celebration. And we had to work our tails off to get anybody to come.

Those who came always seemed to love it. But slowly over the years it dawned on me that if we had to work so hard to get people to come, maybe they didn't value our training events as much as we thought.

So we cut back.

And no one complained, even those who seemed to enjoy the previous meetings the most.

We've since cut back even more drastically on our training events, without any falloff in the quality of our groups and with a marked increase in the raw number and long-term retention of our leaders.

Later we'll look in greater depth at how we train leaders and hosts. But here's a quick overview of how we currently limit their time commitment.

We now have just two major meetings a year. The first is a Friday night fall kickoff designed to recharge and refocus everyone as we restart after our summer break. The other is a halftime refocus that takes place in January. Leaders and hosts also meet for training and updating two other times a year—but these meetings are now held simultaneously with our worship services, meaning they no longer demand an extra night out.

Another way we've cut down on the number of meetings for our leaders has been by providing weekly training and insider information through an audio recording that can be picked up on a leaders' CD at any of the weekend services or accessed online.

These are short and to the point, in line with our belief that training is usually more effective when it's dripped in over the long haul rather than dumped out all at once.

When we first started providing training tapes (remember the days of cassette tapes?), they were too long and contained too much information. Some even began by suggesting that listeners get a cup of coffee, pull up a chair, and sit down with pen and paper in hand.

But the truth was, nobody sat down with pen and paper. Most listened in the car on their way to work. No doubt, some hit the fast-forward button. Now we know better. Our typical weekly training audios run ten to fifteen minutes max. And we've designed them to be listened to in a multitask environment.

Summer Breaks

Another way we've dealt with the time crunch is to take the summer off. That has some disadvantages. But it's one of the most important reasons why we've been able to keep our people, and especially our leaders and hosts, involved for decades instead of just a couple of years.

Our first session starts in mid-September and goes until just before Christmas. After a couple of weeks off, the second session starts with the new year and continues until Easter. The third session picks up two weeks later and ends right before school lets out.

Frankly, by the end of the third session, some of our leaders are running on fumes. Okay, most of our leaders are running on fumes.

If we asked for a year-round commitment, we'd lose a significant number of leaders and even groups every year. Weekly meetings and the messiness of frontline ministry take their toll. But after a summer away, nearly all our leaders and group members are anxious to get back at it.

The biggest downside of our summer break is that it leaves us with nothing particularly sticky during a time when many new people are moving into the community, looking for a new church home. It means we're not at our best. But it's a price we're willing to pay to stay healthy for the long haul.

In the meantime we use a variety of other programming vehicles to help us connect people during the summer months. That's when we hold most of our North Coast U courses. It's also a great time for special-interest groups—for instance, a road trip for our motorcycle enthusiasts. When we were much smaller, we also hosted a series of churchwide social events.

We even start up some short-term, give-it-a-try growth groups for those who are new to the church. They launch in August and are only four weeks long. But they help cover the relational gap and give new folks a taste of what's ahead in the fall.

I see no indication that our culture's time crunch is about to go away. Seems to me that virtually every time-saver we've come up with only makes life busier. Sure, it speeds up a task or two (like editing this chapter). But it also increases what I'm expected to accomplish (like responding to email whether I'm at home, on the road, or in the office).

Like it or not, we live in an increasingly multitasked world, where most people are unable or unwilling to give us more than two time slots a week. That makes convincing people to participate in or lead a small group a tough task. But it can be done, as evidenced by our 80 percent rate of participation in small groups for over a quarter century.

The secret is to find as many ways as you can to cut the competition and to do away with as many nonessential meetings as possible. It's why I always like to ask, "What would happen if we stopped doing this?"

And why if the answer is, "Not much," or "I don't know," I'm usually willing to give it a shot — right between the eyes.

Chapter 13

Determining Your Primary Purpose

When I hang around and listen to leaders in the small group movement, I'm amazed at the diversity of opinion as to what the primary purpose of a small group ought to be. Not only is there no universal standard or any sense of widespread agreement; when you read the books, attend the seminars, or simply check out small group websites, you'll find a plethora of mutually exclusive goals and purposes.

Some see small groups as the ideal vehicle for discipleship. Some think they're the perfect tool for evangelism. Some view them as the secret to unlimited church growth. Still others use them to shepherd the flock, administrate the church, provide for deep Bible study, or produce an environment that fosters no-holds-barred sharing and prayer. And then there are always those who just want everyone to have some friends.

With so many competing viewpoints and paradigms, it's essential that the primary purpose for your small group ministry be agreed on before launch and then carefully and continually articulated from that point onward. Otherwise everyone ends up using a different measuring rod to determine the effectiveness of the groups. And when that happens, it's nearly impossible to keep everyone happy and on track.

At North Coast we made it clear from the beginning that our primary purpose would be to foster significant Christ-centered relationships. Everything else was secondary.

That has helped us keep our eye on our North Star and avoid knee-jerk shifts in focus or emphasis every time someone points out something we aren't doing well or could do better if we made some changes in the way we run our groups.

While you might prefer a different purpose for your groups (and may indeed have had great success pursuing it), let's take a look at why we chose to make the development of significant relationships our primary purpose, why you might want to consider it for your own ministry, and how that decision impacts everything we do.

Aligning the Mission

It all starts with our mission. We describe it this way: *Making disciples in a healthy church environment.* It's our way of expressing that when it comes to ministry, both task and health are equally important.

Like me, you've probably come across your share of high-powered ministries where boatloads of people come to Christ but nearly as many limp out the back door, overworked, burnt out, and used up.

You've also no doubt seen other churches that pride themselves on being spiritually and doctrinally healthy but never lead anyone to Christ except an occasional "nice" neighbor or a member's child.

I liken it to Wall Street and the LA Fitness Club. On Wall Street you'll find some amazing resumes and lots of people who've done the *task* part of life (read that as making disciples) incredibly well. Yet on closer examination, you'll find that many of them have sacrificed their physical, emotional, and relational health to get the job done. It may make for an impressive obituary — but hardly a life well lived.

In a similar way, you can go down to any local fitness club and find plenty of body beautifuls who are doing the *health* part of life (read that as spiritual health) incredibly well. They're buffed out, patched up, and pumped full of the latest nutritional supplements. Their life goal seems to be living longer and looking younger than the rest of us. Yet when it's all said and done, most won't have accomplished anything of significance, unless you consider looking younger and living a few extra years a worthy life goal.

Not wanting to fail at our primary task of fulfilling the Great Commission or sacrifice our spiritual health, we crafted a mission statement that incorporated both. And to make sure it didn't become a meaningless slogan stashed in a drawer somewhere, we also came up with a series of benchmarks to measure how well we're doing in each area.

Making Disciples

To measure the task of making disciples, we monitor three basic steps in the discipleship process:

1. Enlisting new followers into God's kingdom
2. Training them how to live the Christian life
3. Equipping them and deploying them into service

With a little work, it's not that hard to keep track of how many people come to Christ, how many stick, whether we're teaching people how to live the Christian life, and how many have been equipped and deployed into kingdom service (both inside and outside the walls of the church).

Staying Healthy

It's been much harder to measure overall health. But by monitoring five vital signs, or key indicators, of spiritual health, we've been able to stay on top of it.

VITAL SIGNS OF HEALTH

WORD • WORSHIP • WITNESS • WARMTH • WORK

While these five traits are somewhat arbitrary, in the sense that they could be squeezed into a list of three or expanded into a list of ten or twelve, we believe they include all the marks of a healthy church.

In no particular order (since vital signs are all equally vital), the five areas we monitor are:

- Word
- Worship
- Witness
- Warmth
- Works

As you noticed, they all start with *W*. That's because those of us who developed this list went to Bible school and took the preaching course that teaches you how to hide boring content behind clever alliteration. We did well, didn't we?

The *W* we call Warmth took the biggest stretch to come up with and still needs the most explaining today. It simply means the experience of significant Christian relationships — the kind where we're known, cared for, and held accountable when necessary.

To ensure that we remain continually focused on these five *W*s and stay ruthlessly honest in our evaluation of how we're doing, every program and ministry is assigned a primary purpose that fits one (or at the most two) of these *W*s.

For instance, our weekend worship services are designed to make sure we're healthy in Word and Worship. I don't worry that the anonymity of a large crowd hinders significant relationships (Warmth). And likewise, while we have plenty of people come to Christ (Witness) and have lots of people serving behind the scenes (Work), these are not the lenses through which we judge the success or failure of our weekend services.

On the other hand, our community service ministry and our "weekend of service" (a weekend when we cancel all worship services to send everyone out to serve in the community) are designed primarily for Witness and Work. So we don't worry when no one cracks open a Bible.

One of the most common mistakes I find churches making when it comes to ministry programming is that in every meeting and program they have, they try to accomplish everything they're called to do.

This inevitably dilutes the original purpose and focus of the meeting or program. Ministry is essentially a zero-sum game. Adding a new element or purpose always means taking time, energy, and focus away from the original areas of emphasis. It's simply impossible to do everything at once.

Yet that's precisely what I see happening in small group ministries time after time. Small groups start out with one agenda and quickly add three or four more.

The Need for Warmth

Have you noticed that whenever someone attempts to offer an apologetic for small groups, the first thing they point to is the dearth of close relationships in our increasingly mobile and rootless society? It's almost always offered as the chief reason why we need small groups in our churches.

Everyone quotes from the same set of surveys, studies, and factoids: Americans are more relationally isolated than ever. We're "cocooning" and "bowling alone." Twenty-five percent of us claim that we have zero close friends. Half of us claim no more than two—and that includes immediate family members. And so on.

I don't disagree. That's why we started our own small groups. Even when we were a small church with a decidedly "family feel," we knew that the majority of our people would never move beyond casual acquaintances without them.

But once we drank the small group Kool-Aid and started developing our own groups, I began to notice a strong disconnect between rhetoric and practice. All the experts said we needed to start small groups because we lived in an unconnected culture. But most of the things they wanted us to focus on and do with our groups had little to nothing to do with building relationships.

It's a disconnect I still feel today. See if you don't agree.

Mission Creep

Despite the nearly universal emphasis on the need for life-on-life relationships, virtually every small group model out there has much less to do with creating and sustaining long-term significant relationships than with promoting evangelism and church growth, or shepherding the flock.

Even so-called affinity-based small groups seldom focus on authentic and sticky relationships as a goal. More often than not, affinity is simply the organizing principle. But the group's primary focus and ultimate goal is usually something else altogether.

Such common practices as having an empty chair waiting to be filled, asking groups to continually divide and multiply, and assigning people into groups based on geography have little to do with fostering long-term significant relationships. Fact is, in many cases these things make it harder to maintain ongoing relationships.

That's not to say that evangelism, church growth, missional outreach, and shepherding the flock aren't important. It is to say that perhaps they can be better done in other settings and through other programs, leaving small groups to do what they do best.

Here is my bottom-line concern. If we focus our small groups on evangelism, deeper discipleship, church growth, or shepherding, when and where will we meet the widespread need for significant and sticky relationships that launched our small group ministries in the first place? What will we use to take their place?

I've never found a better tool for creating and sustaining authentic Christian relationships than healthy small groups. That's why, despite nearly constant pressure to add a new initiative or veer off in the direction of some other good and important aspect of ministry, I've refused to let our original focus on relationships be sacrificed on the altar of other important tasks, no matter how essential they may be.

Measuring Success

Practically speaking, this means that when it comes to measuring the success of our sermon-based small groups, I look primarily at the quality of the relationships within the groups and at the level of membership retention from one session to the next.

To measure the quality of relationships, I look for stories of mortgages and rents being paid, meals provided, hospital visits, holidays and vacations spent together, encouragement, and tough confrontations. All in all, the same stuff I'd look for in a healthy extended family.

That doesn't mean I'm not into deeper Bible study, evangelism, or worship. It just means that given the choice between a small group system that features a lighter Bible study but connects lots of people relationally and another model that promotes deeper study or more intimate worship but only works for the faithful few, I'll go with the more accessible format every time.

The best way to see the most people grow deeper in their walk with God is not by having a few folks gather for an in-depth study and worship. It's by having lots of folks tightly velcroed to other Christians and the Scriptures for the long haul.

What Revisioning and Reengineering Really Means

The clearest sign that many of our popular small group models aren't working as advertised is the constant level of revisioning and reengineering that goes on in the movement and within our churches.

The turnovers in leadership and changes in direction remind me of a giant game of musical chairs. Even the most prominent churches and those that provide conferences on how to do small groups keep changing horses and riders midstream, often swapping one model or leader for another.

Let's be honest. Things that work well and fulfill their purpose don't go through a series of major revisions and reengineering—which are simply code words for "We're starting all over again."

To my thinking, the major culprits have been an idealism that expects small groups to do too much, and a form of mission creep that has them quickly veering off to chase everything except their original purpose.

Unfortunately, every time that happens, the congregation's confidence in the credibility of the leadership and in the effectiveness of small groups is eroded, making each restart harder than the last one.

In contrast, by staying fearlessly focused on sticky relationships, our sermon-based small groups have been able to provide powerful, life-changing relationships for decades without the need to revision or reengineer. And they've done so despite radical changes in the size, complexity, and makeup of both our ministry and our community.

Chapter 14

Entry Points and Escape Routes

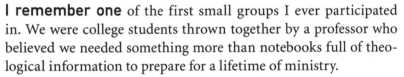

I remember one of the first small groups I ever participated in. We were college students thrown together by a professor who believed we needed something more than notebooks full of theological information to prepare for a lifetime of ministry.

There were seven of us in the group. The idea was to meet weekly to pray, share, and support each other in our studies, life, and ministry.

I hated it.

First, I already had a group of friends who were meeting those needs in my life. Second, while on the surface it may have appeared as if we had a lot in common (our commitment to Jesus, our preparations for ministry, a similar age, a shared struggle with the frustrating nuances of the Greek language), in reality we didn't connect.

I'm not sure why.

Maybe they thought I was too rebellious and irreverent. I know I thought a couple of them were too wide-eyed and gullible. I liked my rock and roll loud — really loud. The guy next to me thought anything with a beat belonged to the Devil, even if it had Christian words tacked on. Then there was the kid whose voice dropped two octaves and whose vocabulary suddenly became Shakespearean every time he prayed.

I once called God "Dude." He called him, "Oh most holy and precious Lord."

I was glad they were all Christians. The evangelist in me was thrilled that they had their eternity squared away. But I have to admit I was also quite happy to know that heaven is big—really big.

Now, imagine this happening not in a group that a professor assigned me to but in one I've signed up for myself. And imagine that we're supposed to meet for an entire year.

Odds are, I'll do exactly the same thing I did with my professor's group. I'll find a way to weasel out of the commitment. And once I finally extricate myself, it will be a cold day in a place where I don't plan to ever go before I try another one.

The Weasel Factor

Yet that's exactly the way many churches structure their small group ministries. In the mistaken belief that our unity in Christ and a sincere commitment to spiritual growth will trump any personality clashes or relational near misses, we put people together by affinity or neighborhood and throw away the key.

But people won't stick with things or groups that are uncomfortable. Maybe they should. But they don't. So they weasel out.

If you've ever been weaseled on or been the weasel yourself, you know it's a miserable experience filled with lame excuses, awkward silences, averted glances, and ofttimes a giant elephant in the room. Is it any wonder that people who've gone through it once seldom sign up to go through it again?

What's the best way to avoid the weasel factor? Make it unnecessary. Give people pain-free off-ramps and easy escape routes. Make them plentiful.

We do that by limiting our small group sessions to just ten weeks. We also give new members the first three weeks to decide whether to opt in for the rest of the session or bail out. No questions asked, no drive-by guiltings.

I'm often asked how in the world we can develop life-changing sticky relationships in just ten weeks. Fact is, we can't. But by stringing together enough ten-week sessions, we end up with something much deeper than we'd ever get with a mere six-month or one-year commitment—and very little weaseling.

Just Ten Weeks

The beauty of a short ten-week study session is that it automatically provides quick access to both on-ramps and off-ramps. Yet it also lasts long enough to allow a slow-jelling group time to connect.

I always tell people new to our church that it may take three or four groups before they find one that feels like home. I liken it to finding a new church in a new town. Some people hit the jackpot on the first try. Most don't. Those who visit numerous churches before settling in aren't flaky or uncommitted. They're just a little pickier.

I don't want us to do anything that makes those who don't enjoy their first attempt at a small group feel guilty or uncommitted. I want them to know it's okay. I want them to know they aren't alone. I want them to keep trying until we get it right.

To make it easier on those who want to opt out (and on those left behind), at the end of each ten-week session we ask everyone to fill out a brief evaluation form. It includes a question about their plans for the next quarter. There are three options:

1. I will continue in this group.
2. I will be taking a break.
3. I will try a new group.

In reality, the vast majority stick with the group they're already in. Only a miniscule percentage leave their groups. But for those who do, it's not miniscule. It's a big deal. By making it simpler and socially acceptable to make the change, we greatly decrease the odds of a one-and-done experience and increase the odds that they'll give another group a shot.

Frankly, this is a major contributor (though mostly unsung) to the incredibly high percentage of small group involvement we've been able to maintain over the years. I'm convinced that we'd have a lot less people velcroed to our church and to one another if we'd made the mistake of making it too tough for people to get out of a group they didn't want to be in.

How Groups Grow Deeper

An easy-out philosophy doesn't mean a lower commitment level. It actually creates more opportunities for greater commitment.

But just as the relationships in a group can't be forced, neither can spiritual depth. Ultimately, all we can do is provide an environment conducive to deeper spiritual relationships among group members. After that, it's up to the Holy Spirit to do his stuff according to a timetable that fits his plan (or in the case of resistant saints, at a pace at which they're willing to be led).

Groups must be allowed to grow deeper at their own speed. When pushed or coerced to go too deep too fast, people will inevitably head for the exits.

That's why we don't do much to push groups to move deeper more quickly. It's better to back off and let them get there eventually than to lose the chance altogether. I liken our patience to Jesus' promise that a bruised reed he will not break and a smoldering wick he will not snuff out.[7] It's all about helping the weak cross the finish line.

In almost every case, they will get there in due time. That's because sooner or later life will happen. And when it does, things get real—real fast.

An unexpected trial or a significant crisis changes everything. Groups that were previously static, superficial, or even bored with one another go deep practically overnight. Forced to become the hands and feet of Jesus, they live out the body of Christ metaphor as a daily reality. And when they do, "my small group" quickly becomes "my family."

The beauty of this laid-back, trust-the-Holy-Spirit-to-do-exactly-what-Jesus-said-he-would-do approach is that it takes the pressure off our leadership team. We don't have to produce elaborate schemes, structures, and processes to produce spirituality. All we have to do is provide an environment where people are connected closely enough and long enough for life to happen and for God to show up. It's organic and simple. And it works.

And it's another reason why I love a ten- to twelve-week format. It's not so long that people have to weasel out, and it's long enough for life to happen in a way that bonds the group together.

When Life Doesn't Happen

Trial and crisis are easily the most powerful forces for bringing a group to a deep spiritual level. But just meeting together for multiple ten-week sessions will bring most groups to a deeper level, even in the absence of a life crisis.

By the end of a typical ten-week session, most groups have already bonded socially. But they've probably not yet developed the trust that leads to full disclosure and authenticity. That usually takes a session or two more.

Of course, sometimes it takes longer. If a group has a know-it-all, a class clown, an EGR (extra grace required), or lots of reserved personalities, the process slows down. But eventually even that group will get there.

The path that turns strangers into a tightly knit spiritual family is pretty straightforward. Groups predictably go through the following stages.

It's nearly impossible to skip a step. Trying to speed up the process usually backfires. But the good news is that there is an almost irresistible relational gravity that propels groups down through the list toward authenticity and accountability, if we can just keep them connected long enough for it to happen.

Like many of you, I've experienced the powerful pull of this process in the sports teams, neighborhoods, and work groups I've been a part of. I also discovered the reason why while working on my doctoral dissertation, "The Impact of a Structured Training Program on the Group Cohesiveness and Job Satisfaction of a Volunteer Leadership Team."

I know—it bored me too.

But in the midst of my research, I came across a series of studies that indicated that the amount of time a group spends together correlates directly to the level of personal appreciation for one another and overall sense of group cohesiveness. In other words, it's not what people do in a group that matters as much as simply staying together for the long haul.

In our sermon-based small groups, the sermons and questions are important. They keep us focused on God. But it's the process as a whole, much more than any particular sermon series or set of questions, that creates spiritually deep relationships.

And that brings up the whole issue of trying to align our sermon series with the beginning and ending points of our small group study sessions.

Sermon Series Alignment

It's often assumed that with sermon-based small groups, every sermon series has to be juggled to coincide with the beginning and ending of a small group session.

Not so.

Over the years, lots of pastors have told me that they love the idea of sermon-based small groups but can't imagine trying to synchronize every sermon series with a small group calendar. This is especially true of those who are committed to an expositional journey through books of the Bible.

They want the passages to speak for themselves, and they feel it would be unfaithful to the text to truncate a sermon series, or stretch it out an extra three weeks, just to dovetail with the start or ending of a small group.

I understand their concern. Actually, I share it.

But in reality, there is no need to worry about aligning a sermon series with your small group calendar. I hardly ever try to bring the two together. In fact, we often start new groups (even our major fall kickoff) in the middle or near the end of a sermon series.

If the real power for deeper relationships and spiritual growth is found in the *process* of spending time together grappling with the implications of the previous weekend's sermon and text, it doesn't matter all that much which sermon it is or where it fits in any given series.

> Bite-sized commitments can produce long-term relationships. The secret is to string them together for the long haul.

Chapter 15

Why Dividing Groups Is a Dumb Idea

Dividing groups is a dumb idea.

I know. *Dumb* is a strong word. But now that I've got your attention, let's see if you don't come to the same conclusion after we've looked more closely at this strategy's underlying rationale and unintended consequences.

For decades it's been an unquestioned canon within the small group movement that healthy groups multiply by continually growing and splitting into new groups. Groups that stay together too long are considered stagnant. Those that fail to aggressively add new members are written off as uncommitted to the Great Commission. Any group that insists on remaining together gets tagged as selfish.

Admittedly, dividing to multiply is an idea that looks good on paper. It sounds great at leadership conferences. It's organic, mirroring the cellular growth of the human body. It offers the potential for unlimited kingdom expansion. It encourages people to reach out to the lost. It forces new leaders to step up and take the reins.

No wonder most small group gurus, church consultants, and pastors with a passion for evangelism and church growth swear by the concept.

But what about those who are in a small group? Fact is, they tend to see it differently—very differently. They generally hate the idea. They don't swear by it. They swear at it.

If you don't believe me, start asking people in churches where small groups are pressured to multiply by dividing. Ask them what they think of the empty chair they're supposed to fill during each session, and the expectation that they'll help grow the church by growing and then dividing their group.

Except for pastors, staff members, and church leaders who are professionally responsible for the growth of the church, you'll find that hardly anyone thinks it's a good idea—especially those who are fortunate enough to find a group filled with significant relationships.

To most of them it makes no sense at all. After finally finding some people with whom they've closely connected, they don't want to split up and roll the relational dice once again.

It's too risky. It's painful. It's even a little bit cruel.

I've asked many of these folks why they don't simply dig in their heels and say no.

Some tell me they have, only to be written off as uncooperative and spiritually self-centered. Others tell me they've tried to raise their concerns but no one seems to listen. Most tell me they don't want to be branded as unspiritual or selfish, so they shrug their shoulders and go along with the program or quietly drop out at the first opportunity.

While many church leaders are quick to chalk up such responses as spiritually immature, shortsighted, or indicative of a lack of commitment to the larger cause of Christ, I think that's a mistake.

It's not that these people are resistant to the Great Commission or don't want their churches to grow. It's simply that for many of them, their small group is the first time they've experienced the authentic and transparent relationships they've always been told Christians should have with one another. It's understandable they're reluctant to let it go. They know the odds of finding it right away in another group aren't too high.

Unintended Consequences

Actually, dividing to multiply can (and often does) work in the short run. But it usually takes only a couple of cycles before the process starts to lose steam and then stalls out.

Trying to multiply a small group ministry by division is a lot like bulking up on steroids. After an initial burst of newfound strength and muscle, the unintended consequences start to show up. And when they do, it isn't pretty.

That's one of the major reasons why so many small group ministries built on this pattern seem to go through a significant revisioning or reengineering every three to five years. Not realizing the negative effects of continually dividing their groups, churches keep retooling them with the latest hot curriculum, new idea, or novel structure, only to do it again a few years later.

Here are just a few of the most significant problems that dividing to multiply creates.

Relational Overload

As we saw earlier, people are a lot like Legos. Some of us have lots of connectors, and some have few. But once those connectors are filled, our capacity for close and significant relationships is maxed out.

We're friendly, but we don't connect.

We can't.

We're already relationally full.

Small group ministries that continually divide their existing groups to form new groups ignore this principle. It's inevitable that after a few cycles of splitting healthy groups, the quality of the relationships within the new groups starts to dissipate.

That's because members who agree to keep spinning off into new groups have fewer and fewer connectors available with the start of each new group. They may have plenty of *physical* openings in their group, but they usually have few if any *emotional* openings in their lives.

The result is a predictable clash of expectations. The newest members join hoping to develop significant relationships. But most of the holdovers aren't looking to fill a relational vacuum. They just want a Bible study with a few new friends.

That explains why those who join a group in which half or more of the members come from a previously existing group so often complain that the group is a bit cliquish and hard to break into.

In most cases the problem isn't cliquishness. It's a differing set of relational needs, expectations, and capacities.

Certainly, there are some people who are adept at quickly jettisoning old relationships and adding new ones to their inner circle. Like social butterflies, they thrive in an environment of constantly changing relationships. But most of us aren't very good at it. And most of us have no desire to become good at it.

A Lesson from Camp Pendleton

Another unintended consequence of expecting groups to continually divide and multiply for the good of the cause is that it eventually leads to shallower, not deeper, relationships across the board.

When relationships are predictably transitional, most of us instinctively find ways to avoid or lessen the pain of separation. It's human nature.

Our church is near a marine base known as Camp Pendleton. Thousands of military families live on base and nearby. Typically, the military moves these families every three years or so, often from West Coast to East Coast. Some families thrive on it. They love the adventure. Others struggle with it. They hate the constant disruption and inability to put down roots.

But I've noticed something that both groups have in common. After a couple of cross-country moves, they learn to keep new relationships at a safe distance.

It's not that they aren't friendly. They are. But they also know it won't be long until it's time to pick up and move again. So rather than set themselves up to be hurt too badly when the time comes to say good-bye, they tend to keep most relationships at arm's length — close but not too close. It hurts less that way.

In much the same way, church members who repeatedly experience the death of their small group to start a new group begin to operate in a self-protective mode. They learn to keep relationships at a safe level — one that won't cause them too much hurt when the group disbands.

Mayberry in San Diego

The high mobility of our society has created a culture without roots. The size of our cities, communities, and social institutions (today's midsized church would have been considered huge throughout most of history) has created a culture of anonymity.

Combine rootlessness with anonymity, and we have an environment in which significant long-term relationships are hard to come by — even for Christians well connected within their church.

Yet the New Testament assumes we are living out our faith in the context of relationships that are close enough to carry out the thirty-plus "one anothers" it commands.

What to do? No worry. Small groups will ride to the rescue.

At least that's the rhetoric.

In most churches, when small groups are first launched, they're sold as the panacea for the isolation and rootlessness so many of us feel, the perfect tool to provide true community and authentic relationships. We're told they'll make it harder to hide and pretend, while at the same time providing a place for genuine acceptance and the relational stability we intuitively long for.

And for those who try out small groups, this is not just rhetoric. It's fact. They actually work that way.

But when ministry leaders convince people to join a small group to counteract the relational bankruptcy of our culture, and then immediately turn around and tell them that if they love Jesus, they'll split the group right after it jells, the leaders are sending a mixed message at best, a dishonest one at worst.

Either people need the relational stability and deep relationships of a small group or they don't. Church leaders can't have it both ways, pushing people into groups to overcome the ills of a transient, impersonal society and then asking them to ditch the solution not long after it starts to work, just to grow the church larger.

At North Coast, we decided at the beginning that our sermon-based small groups would hold to their original purpose of creating significant and sticky relationships. So rather than ask healthy groups to divide, we not only allow them to stay together as long as they like; we encourage it.

Some have been together for decades. Contrary to what many would predict, they haven't grown stale. But their members have grown older together with a dignity and beauty reminiscent of a time when communities had stability and people had roots.

To me, that's a good thing.

If you ask them, it's a great thing.

It's a little bit of Mayberry, USA, in the middle of a hectic and relationally shallow culture known as Southern California.

Fresh Blood

This doesn't mean that these groups don't have the opportunity to add fresh blood or that we end up with lots of unhealthy groups hanging around forever.

Fact is, sick groups don't last. Long before we have to kill one, it usually dies of attrition. People don't stay in groups that are dysfunctional, shallow, or relationally challenged. They take the first exit ramp they see.

As for fresh blood, even our longest-lasting groups get their share of it, thanks to the normal transitions of life. People change jobs, move, retire, face other life changes, and even die. When something like that happens, it creates an opening that's filled by someone who brings a fresh perspective and an inevitable change in the relational dynamic of the group.

But unlike the relational white water that occurs when half the members of a group are new and half are holdovers from a previous group, the slight ripples caused by the periodic addition of a few new members make for easy assimilation.

It's much like a friendly small town welcoming a new family every couple of years, which is a far cry from splitting the town in half every few years.

Seeding New Groups

I'm often asked, "If groups aren't pushed to divide and are allowed to stay together as long as they like, how is it possible to create new groups fast enough to meet the needs of a growing church — especially a rapidly growing church?"

The answer lies in two strategies: starting new groups for new people, and hiving off leaders rather than dividing entire groups. New groups for new people are relatively easy to start and quick to bond, because most everyone comes with a strong desire to connect. Of course, these groups need someone who is not so new to lead the way. And that's where hiving off leaders comes in.

We ask every small group leader in our existing groups to appoint an apprentice leader who will head up their group at least once a quarter. Then, at the end of each quarter, we contact the leaders and ask if anyone in their group (apprentice or not) is ready to step up and lead their own group.

If one of the leaders suggests a name, we ask for permission to recruit that person as a potential leader. But if the current leader says, "No, this isn't a good time for me, our group, or the prospective leader," we move on. No pressure. No drive-by guiltings.

If the current leader says, "Okay," we contact the potential leader (after vetting them with the ministry staff) and ask if they'd like to step out and lead a group. Again, if their answer is, "No," or, "Not now," we move on. But if it's, "Yes! I'm honored you asked," we've got the leader we're looking for.

Without fail, we've found that this process of waiting until people feel called of the Spirit provides the leaders we need — even during times of hypergrowth. And it does so without creating a ministry culture in which key positions are filled grudgingly, out of undue pressure and guilt.

I'm convinced that the boom-and-bust cycle of small groups, the constant revisioning and reengineering that so many churches experience, could be easily stopped if those of us who lead small group ministries would simply remember why we started them in the first place and then ruthlessly stick to our original mission: helping people develop authentic and transparent Christian relationships.

Chapter 16

Finding and Developing Leaders

My friend Bobb Biehl likes to say that every organization eventually becomes a direct reflection of its leadership, whether for good or for bad.[8]

I think he's right. It doesn't matter whether it's an entire church, an ancillary ministry, or a small group Bible study; the principle holds true with uncanny accuracy. Tell me the quality of your leaders, and I'll tell you the quality of your ministry, program, or small group.

That's why an essential part of developing and maintaining a healthy small group ministry is finding the right kind of leaders. It's not enough to simply assign a leader to each group and hope for the best — or worse yet, hand the reins to anyone who happens to volunteer. Instead we need a reliable process for identifying and recruiting the best possible leaders. And it has to be realistic. It can't raise the bar so high that no one qualifies or make the training process so long and laborious that no one finishes.

That process demands a clear understanding of the type of person who typically makes the best leader. It also demands a dependable grid for evaluating who fits in and who doesn't. Here are some things that will help you create it.

What to Look For

By definition, a small group ministry has a high leader-to-participant ratio. While that can make the recruitment and development of quality leaders seem like a daunting task, in reality the odds of selecting the right kind of leaders can be greatly increased by simply focusing on two key traits.

Spiritual Warmth

The most important trait to look for is spiritual warmth. By that I mean a growing relationship with Jesus. It's absolutely essential. No amount of giftedness, knowledge, or people skills can compensate for its absence.

But don't confuse spiritual warmth with spiritual maturity. They are not the same.

Spiritual warmth is characterized by obedience to the light we have. It can be found in a new Christian. It can be found in someone with a sketchy understanding of the Bible. Spiritual maturity, on the other hand, is different. It's godliness with a track record. It's equated with a solid grasp of Scripture, significant time in the faith, and a short list of other factors that varies from one tribe of Christians to another.

You can see the distinction between spiritual warmth and spiritual maturity in the apostle Paul's approach to ministry. When it came to selecting elders for an established church, his standards were high. He insisted on spiritual maturity. The qualifications he spelled out in 1 Timothy 3 and Titus 1 are not easily attained.

But when it came to finding leaders for a new church, Paul's standards were much lower. No assessment tools. No church planter boot camps. No well-funded endowments. Instead he simply went into a town and preached the gospel until he was jailed, beaten, chased out, or otherwise called to a new location. Left behind would be a new church filled with (and usually led by) those who had only recently come to Christ. Clearly, no one was mature yet. But they were ready and willing to grow. They had spiritual warmth. That was enough to start a church and hold it together.

Only later, after enough time had passed to produce some spiritual maturity, did Paul or his emissaries come back and appoint elders to authoritative positions of general oversight.

Pastors and church leaders sometimes complain that they can't find enough spiritually qualified leaders for their small group ministry. I don't buy it. Most of the time, it's a case of insisting on spiritual maturity when spiritual warmth would do. Raising the bar too high practically guarantees a scarcity of "qualified" leaders. If spiritual maturity becomes our benchmark, there will never be enough small group leaders in a growing ministry.

Perhaps a stagnant church filled with longtime Christians might claim to have lots of spiritually mature leaders. But then I'd have to ask, How mature are they if everyone knows how to quote the Great Commission but no one knows how to carry it out?

One of the great strengths of the sermon-based small group model is that it demands a less skilled and less biblically literate leader. It's a lot easier to facilitate a discussion of the previous weekend's sermon than it is to lead a group through a typical small group curriculum. All you need is spiritual warmth. You don't need spiritual maturity.

Relational Warmth

The second essential trait in a good leader is relational warmth. People with low social skills or low emotional intelligence make lousy small group leaders.

I like to ask, Is this person likable? Do people enjoy being around them? Where do they fit on the it-would-be-fun-to-have-dinner-with-you scale?

This doesn't mean that every good leader has to ooze charisma, be extroverted, or make their living in sales. Introverts and quiet types can make great leaders. But let's face it: Those who don't know how to play well with others quickly empty the sandbox. Those who are constantly negative or whiny end up alone. Those who demand too much attention get ignored.

When we allow people who lack relational warmth to lead a group, they kill it. It doesn't matter if they've got great theological training, can quote a ton of Bible verses, sincerely love God, or desperately want to lead a group. If they're not good with people, they'll kill it.

Worse, those who join their group unaware end up in a relational purgatory. If they don't take the option of bailing out in the first few weeks or try to hang in there to see if it gets better, they end up feeling stuck, having committed to an entire session. While there may be an end in sight, it can't come quickly enough; and whether they stick it out or drop out, they're usually lost for good. They'll seldom try another group.

While I've yet to find a surefire test or single trait that guarantees relational warmth, I sure recognize its absence. Everyone does.

But here's the problem. Most Christian leaders recoil from acting on a negative gut feeling without some hard facts to back it up. It doesn't seem fair or right. Didn't Jesus give us all a second chance? How can we not give someone a first chance? And what if we're wrong? So we let these people lead, even though we know they won't succeed.

We think we're being kind. But it's anything but kind to knowingly send someone off to fail. And it's hardly kind to the people who unwittingly sign up for a group we knew all along would be awful. Ignoring a lack of relational warmth is a mistake every time. Trust your gut. I bet you've never been wrong on this one yet. You won't be wrong in the future, either.

Whom to Avoid

Along with those who lack a growing relationship with Christ and those who are socially challenged, there are two other traits that predictably make for a bad leader. Yet, strangely, in some circles people with these two traits not only become leaders; they're fast-tracked for leadership, almost always with disastrous consequences. Here's what to watch out for.

Hyperspiritual God-Talkers

Anyone who is hyperspiritual, constantly peppering their speech with God-talk, makes for a terrible small group leader. I know it's hard to blackball someone who appears to be exceptionally zealous for God. But if you don't, you'll regret it.

You know the type. They have all the outward symbols of spirituality. They're committed, a bit fanatical, mildly condescending. They usually know their Bible incredibly well and are quick to let everyone know. They have a verse or Christian cliché for every situation.

Frankly, some are spiritual losers, nothing more than modern-day Pharisees — impressive on the outside but rotting on the inside. Others are the real deal, genuinely sincere Christians who don't realize how they come across. But when it comes to leading a group, it doesn't matter. Both will drive people away. The Pharisees will kill the group with hypocrisy. The real deals will kill it with intimidation.

A hyperspiritual leader squashes any sense of authenticity or honesty in a group. Once they start spouting off, everyone else shuts up and begins to play the let's-pretend-I've-got-it-all-together game. Those who can't (or won't) play the game drop out. The rest simply bury any unacceptable thoughts, ideas, or spiritual struggles. All the good things that a small group is supposed to provide disappear, replaced by banal happy talk and empty platitudes.

Keeping God-talkers at bay is not easy. Some folks in your church won't understand why someone so obviously on fire for God is kept at arm's length. The God-talkers will wonder why they haven't been asked to lead a group yet. Some will get hurt and angry. Some will leave.

Let them go.

You'll be glad you did.

So will the people in your small groups.

Single-Issue Crusaders

Another kind of leader who will destroy a group is the single-issue crusader. It doesn't really matter what the issue is. If someone sees the world through just one narrow lens, it won't be long until they try to force everyone else in the group to join their crusade.

As C. S. Lewis once noted, the progression of a crusader is predictable. What starts out as an important part of their devotion to Christ soon becomes the most important part of their devotion to Christ. Then, before long, it's likely to become even more important than their devotion to Christ.[9]

That makes it almost impossible for a single-issue crusader to appropriately deal with legitimate differences in the body of Christ. It doesn't matter if the differences are centered on a gray area of theology, stem from our imperfect understanding of Scripture, or reflect a new Christian's lack of a biblical worldview. The single-issue crusader won't rest until everyone has been squeezed into their mold.

Those who unwittingly end up in a crusader's group respond in one of three ways: They line up in lockstep, they cower in the corner, or they leave. Most will leave. Few if any will ever come back and try a small group again.

The Best and Worst Fishing Pools

As important as it is to know *what* to look for, it's equally important to know *where* to look. Some fishing pools yield far more of a catch than others. Here's what we've learned about the best and worst places to look for potential small group leaders.

The Best Fishing Pools

The best fishing pools are usually found within the groups you already have. They contain people who understand what you're trying to do. Not only that, if they've been around for a while and are willing to step up to leadership, they also *like* what you're doing and will do their best to replicate it.

As mentioned earlier, we ask every leader to appoint an apprentice leader. This provides us with a constant pool of potential recruits. But we've also recruited many excellent leaders who never served in the role of an apprentice. The key prerequisite to being a leader is not a stint as an apprentice; it's a firsthand experience in one of our groups. That's the only way to ensure that they get what we're trying to do and buy into our core values and methods.

Lots of people think they're ready to step into a ministry role after merely hearing about what we do. They love our underlying philosophy and claim it's what they've always been looking for. Sometimes they convince me, especially when they come with a strong ministry background and credentials. But they're never ready.

It's not that they are disingenuous. They honestly think they've got it. So do I. But what neither of us understands at the time is that we're using the same words with different dictionaries. Until someone actually experiences what goes on, they can't help but read their past experiences and definitions into the words I use. It's the only reference they have. That's why they need to be in *one* of our groups before leading, no matter what giftedness or background they bring to the table.

Obviously, this fishing pool won't work for someone who is just starting to build a sermon-based small group ministry. People who have experienced what you are trying to do don't exist in your church yet. It also won't work in a major turnaround situation. If the current small group ministry is so dysfunctional that it needs a total overhaul, those who are already in a group will probably be a liability. They're predisposed to continue doing what they've always done — the very things that killed off the ministry.

In both of these situations (the start-up and the ministry in need of major reengineering), your best fishing pool might well be found among those who have *never* been in a small group before. They will bring far less baggage and preconceived ideas to the process. What they lack in experience, they'll make up in teachableness. It's always much easier to mold a new leader who doesn't already "know everything" than to mold one who comes in with all the answers.

The Worst Fishing Pools

There are some fishing pools you'll want to avoid. Surprisingly, one of the worst fishing pools for recruiting successful small group leaders is found among those who previously held a leadership position in another church or served in a parachurch ministry.

Not that there is anything wrong with either of these. But I've learned the hard way that when such people are allowed to take the reins of leadership without first having been in one of our small groups, it makes for a bad fit.

That's because those who previously served in leadership at another church almost always think their old church's way is the best way. No surprise, since as leaders they helped mold and shape the way things were done. That means they often (not always, but often enough to make it an issue) come with a strong bias for doing everything the way they did it at their previous church, and with a subtle resistance to the ways we do it here. Handing them the reins before knowing for sure that they understand and buy into what we're doing tends to create problems down the road.

As for those who come out of a parachurch ministry, they too tend to bring some baggage. They almost always share a strong passion for the singular focus of the ministry they served in. That's why they joined it. Whether it's evangelism, discipleship, mercy ministries, or something else, it's the torch they carry.

That can make it difficult for them to see ministry through the eyes of a local church. Whereas a parachurch ministry by calling is narrowly focused, a local church has a much wider constituency and a much broader mandate. It can't zero in on one aspect of ministry or one particular demographic.

I've found that it takes a while for most people who've been immersed in the narrow focus of a parachurch ministry to understand the broad-brush ministry of a local church, no matter how much they love our church. So until they've had the chance to immerse themselves in what we do, the way we do it—and we've had a chance to confirm that they won't be trying to mold everyone into the image of their past ministry—I've found it's best to put them on hold.

Admittedly, that puts some of them off. They don't understand why they have to pay their dues all over again. But once they've experienced what we do and understand why we do it that way, they often become some of our best and most faithful leaders. They bring a maturity and a commitment level that are hard to beat.

The Best and Worst Way to Recruit Leaders

The best way to find new leaders is to ask for recommendations. The worst way is to ask for volunteers.

Asking for Recommendations

Not all recommendations are equal. When they come from a wide swath of the congregation, they can be misleading. Larger groups tend to put forward names of those who are highly visible, personally known, or simply look impressive from a distance. None of which has anything to do with leading a small group well.

On the other hand, when leaders or group members put forward the name of someone who has been in their group, it's a recommendation you can bank on. It's hard to hide a stale walk with God or a relationally challenged personality in a small group setting.

Asking for Volunteers

Asking for volunteers is risky. Too often, it puts you in the awkward position of having to say, "Thanks, but no thanks," to people who step forward with the best of intentions but the worst of qualifications. Once you've asked for help, there is no kind way to say, "I didn't mean *you*."

Asking for volunteers always surfaces a number of folks who love God but don't have the relational skills needed to lead a group. That's because when it comes to self-awareness, socially challenged people don't have any. Most think they're pretty good at getting along with others. Couple that with their high need for attention and affirmation, and you have a bunch of people who are quick to volunteer and hard to turn away.

Another problem with asking for volunteers is that it tends to devalue the role. It sends a message of shortage. It conveys the idea that anyone can do this job. Contrast that with personally recruiting those who have been recommended by fellow group members. That sends a very different message. It elevates the role and conveys the image of honor and prestige.

How to Scare Off Potential Leaders

It's hard to find enough quality leaders if we scare them off before they even start. But that's exactly what happens in many situations in which the recruitment process emphasizes all that a leader *might* be called to do rather than all they *will* be required to do.

Asking for too much too fast makes the task seem overwhelming.

No question, leading a small group can be a tough assignment. At times, it calls for everything from peer counseling to church discipline. It often involves dealing with messy relationships and serious problems. Making hospital visits, organizing support for a member's need, and sharing in a member's tears and heartaches are not easy tasks. When we lay all that out on the front end (or worse, present it as the job description), it scares good people away. They back off, certain they're not up to it. But the fact is, most are. They just don't know it yet.

If I'd known all that God would require of me on the front end of my own ministry, I might have joined Jonah and sailed to Tarshish. But as life and ministry unfolded, things changed. What once seemed impossible or completely undesirable became doable and desirable. Every time God raised the bar of his expectations, the Holy Spirit also provided the internal motivation and power to clear it.

I find the same thing happening over and over with our small group leaders. Once they get involved in ministry and see God using them, they step up to levels of leadership and ministry they never would have thought possible — or been willing to sign up for on the front end. God has a just-in-time delivery system. The power and grace to handle the tough things of leading a small group come when we need them — not one day before. They can't be stored up in a spiritual warehouse somewhere.

That's why telling potential small group leaders ahead of time all they might be called to do is a mistake. It scares them off. It's much better to simply tell them what they will be required to do. Then step back and let life happen. Their group's trials and the Lord's calling will raise the bar. And when the bar is raised, they'll gladly leap over it.

Chapter 17

Training Leaders

When we at North Coast Church began our small group ministry, we fell into a common trap.

We overtrained.

Our goal was to have the best-equipped small group leaders in America. So every fall, we hosted an all-day training event for our leaders and hosts. Every month, we set aside an extra evening for building community and further training. Every week, we provided a cassette tape designed to prepare leaders for the coming week's study.

We thought we were providing top-drawer training. But most of our leaders didn't see it that way. For them, it wasn't great training as much as information overload. They didn't see themselves as the best-trained small group leaders in America. They saw themselves as overscheduled and burnt out on unnecessary meetings.

Truth is, they had no wiggle room in their schedules for an extra night out. It was already a stretch to set aside one night a week for their small group and another evening or lunch hour to prepare to lead their group. Same went for our weekly training tapes. While we assumed that our leaders were sitting down at the kitchen table with pen and paper in hand, ready to dig into some extra biblical insights so they could take their group to a deeper level, in reality we were lucky if they listened to it on their way to work. Or, more truthfully, on their way home from work—two hours before the meeting.

Differing Expectations

Much of the problem stemmed from an all too common disconnect between those of us who are in professional ministry and those of us who volunteer for frontline ministry. We tend to view meetings and time commitments through very different lenses.

Most small group leaders have jobs that demand a minimum of forty to fifty hours a week. Many have a lengthy commute. Some have kids in sports programs that demand hours each day and an entire morning or afternoon each weekend. Some even dare to have a favorite hobby or special interest!

But staff members tend to view job and church involvement as one. A monthly training meeting isn't an extra night out as much as a part of the workweek. In fact, some staff members take the afternoon off as compensation, or sleep in late the next morning to "recover." It's the same for things like our weekly training audio. It may take many hours of prep to put it together, but again it's all part of the job. No one on the ministry staff listens to it during their off hours.

All this tends to make pastors and staff members insensitive to the time crunch that lay leaders feel. Whereas volunteers come to extra training meetings exhausted, staff members come amped up, rested, and ready to do their thing.

The first sign that something was wrong with our approach to training was the increased amount of effort it took to get people to come to the meetings or listen to the weekly audio recordings. We tried adding incentives. We provided higher-quality refreshments. We brought in guest speakers. We made the meetings shorter. We tried drive-by guiltings. We tried making all of our meetings a requirement.

Nothing worked.

Finally it dawned on me that maybe we were asking too much. While our leaders wanted training (at least they told us so), they didn't want it in the way we were providing it. When the time came, they wanted another night at home far more than they wanted the help we were offering.

Now, don't get me wrong. They still needed the training. Some needed it badly. But they weren't going to get it as long as we insisted on offering it in ways they weren't interested in or open to.

So we altered our delivery system.

Bite-Sized Training

Instead of offering training events that demanded a full day, an extra night out, or an evening at the kitchen table, we broke things down into bite-sized pieces.

We still have our fall kickoff. But it just takes an evening now.

We canned our monthly leaders' meetings.

We redesigned the format of our weekly audio training. It's now much shorter. It's designed to be listened to while multitasking, whether driving to work, exercising, or walking the dog. And it can be listened to on a CD or downloaded as a podcast or MP3.

Time Shifting

Another way we've made the training process more accessible is by shifting it to a time when our leaders are already at the church.

I have to admit that this wasn't my idea. In fact, I didn't like it at first. Once our staff bought into the concept of cutting down on the number of meetings, I thought they went way overboard. They wanted to start training our small group leaders during our worship services — in a separate meeting, during my sermon!

Now that's a stupid idea if I ever heard one.

But the more I thought about it, the more sense it made. After all, doesn't the Bible say that the role of a pastor-teacher is to equip the saints for the work of the ministry? And what would better equip our small group leaders for their ministry work than a specialized training session led by one of our pastors? Besides that, they could still hear the sermon. All we had to do was provide them with a CD of the message at the end of their meeting. My initial resistance said more about my own insecurities and desire to have everyone in the sanctuary than about anything else.

So upon further reflection, I said okay.

The result has been greater participation, more effective training, and better leaders — and a few extra empty seats in the worship center for visitors.

Need-Based Training

Turning down the intensity level of our leadership training has not lowered the quality of our leaders or the spiritual impact of our groups. I'd put today's leaders and groups up against any we've ever had. They still get all the training they need. It's just that we now offer it in bite-sized and easily accessible formats. Rather than trying to front-load everything we think leaders might need someday, we offer them "need-based training."

For instance, when a leader comes up against a sticky theological issue or needs to deal with a family in crisis, we're right there, ready to guide them through it.

And they're ready to learn.

In the past, we would have tried to prepare every leader for all of these types of situations ahead of time. As a result, they had some pretty nice notebooks full of Bible verses and leadership principles. But if truth be known, they still called us as soon as the crisis hit, because the notes in their notebooks didn't mean much. Principles taught in a vacuum are like that. They make for nice theory. But most of us have no idea how to put theory into practice, until we're faced with a real-life application. As a result, we take copious notes and then go home and stash our notebooks somewhere, without ever having learned what we've supposedly been taught.

Need-based training saves everyone the hassle. Instead of overloading leaders with information, we just answer the phone when it rings and give them the information and help they need when they need it.

While we now cover much less material in far fewer meetings — and get far better results — there is still a need for some formalized training. Let's take a look at some of the things we think every leader needs to know.

What Every Rookie Needs to Know

Even though our new leaders and hosts come out of an existing group, there are some things they haven't been exposed to, and others they need to be reminded of, that will help them succeed. So we provide them with a special rookie training track. It gives new leaders a quick overview of our basic values and goals. It covers our methods and procedures and explains why we do things a certain way. It ensures that we're all on the same page.

It gives us a chance to prepare new leaders and hosts for some of the most common issues they'll face, from the chatterbox who dominates the meeting to the shy member who hides in the corner, from the theological bulldog with a fierce bark to the member who consistently shows up late or not at all to the couple whose marriage is in crisis.

New leaders also need to know some spiritual basics: the importance and power of prayer, how to maintain their own growing walk with God, and how to biblically confront and handle sin in the group.

To get all this across, we add an extra half-day training session to the fall kickoff. Since new leaders are always a little nervous about how their group will go, it's not hard to get them there. It's a strongly felt need. They want to come. But it's the only extra meeting they have. The rest of the rookie track material is covered during a couple of Sunday morning midquarter training sessions, when they meet separately from the veterans.

Our goal with rookies is twofold. We want to expose them to basic information and processes they'll need to lead a healthy group. And we want them to know we're here to help the moment they're faced with something they either are uncomfortable with or can't handle on their own.

What Every Veteran Needs to Know

While rookies need to know some basic information, veteran leaders and hosts simply need to be reminded that we're available, just a phone call or email away. The content of the veteran training is not particularly important. It has to be relevant and helpful, but it's no big deal. It can cover lots of subjects. It can leave out a lot of stuff as well. What matters most is the process of staying connected.

For instance, the subject matter can spring out of a biblical passage or a book on leadership or small groups. It can relate to an issue some of the groups are facing. It can flow out of something one of our pastors learned at a conference or seminar. As long as the topic is interesting to leaders and applies to their role, they'll get something out of it.

We have some leaders and hosts who've been at it ten, fifteen, twenty years. There's no way we could create a curriculum that projects out that far. And we don't want our longtime leaders to ever feel like they've graduated and no longer need to learn their craft. So we focus on an ever-changing curriculum of hot-button topics and areas of special interest.

Our ultimate goal is simply to keep leaders growing and to stay close enough relationally that when they face a problem, they'll feel free to quickly call for help or advice.

By making our training for leaders and hosts bite-sized, continuous, and convenient, we've been able to give them all the resources they need, without overtaxing their already hectic schedules. It's kept the quality of our small groups at a high level. It's helped our leaders and hosts continue to grow in their role. And it's done so without burning them out or turning them off to the training and support they need.

Chapter 18

Why Cho's Model Didn't Work in Your Church

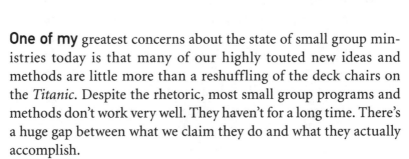

One of my greatest concerns about the state of small group ministries today is that many of our highly touted new ideas and methods are little more than a reshuffling of the deck chairs on the *Titanic*. Despite the rhetoric, most small group programs and methods don't work very well. They haven't for a long time. There's a huge gap between what we claim they do and what they actually accomplish.

In most cases, we know something is wrong. But we don't know what's wrong. So we keep endlessly tweaking things. So much so that, as mentioned earlier, it's become standard practice for any church with a small group ministry to restructure or reengineer the program every few years.

Recently I received two advertisements promoting two different national small group conferences. In each case, the well-known sponsoring churches had once again reorganized and changed out their entire small group pastoral team. Now, less than a couple of years into their newest paradigm, they are offering to show the rest of us how to develop a dynamic and powerful small group ministry. They want me to come and learn their secrets.

Forgive my cynicism. But I don't think so.

Neither does a friend of mine who told me recently that he's finished with these kinds of conferences. He claims that every time he goes, he gets fired up. But every time he goes back for a refresher course, everything has changed.

In reality, most of the changes are cosmetic: a switch from affinity-based groups to neighborhood-based groups and then back again; free market electives followed by a multiyear curriculum and then back to electives. Sometimes the emphasis swings heavily toward outreach. Other times it swings back to discipleship. But in almost every case, the underlying paradigm, assumptions, and basic goals haven't changed. It's been that way for over thirty years.

The Korean Connection

It all goes back to the pervasive and often unrecognized influence of an amazing church in Seoul, South Korea. Under the leadership of Pastor David Yonggi Cho, the Yoido Full Gospel Central Church (affiliated with the Assemblies of God) grew to be the largest church in the world, using a small group, cell-based system as its primary tool for evangelism and church growth.

Cho's model is characterized by three traits.

First, it strongly emphasizes evangelism. Every group is required to have an empty chair that is supposed to be filled with a new Christian before the year is out.

Second, it's based on the idea that the most effective way to bring new Christians into the larger church is to first reach them through a small group.

Third, it promises the potential of unlimited evangelism and church growth, because groups can grow and divide indefinitely — thus providing care and connectedness no matter how large the church gets.

Coming to America

Cho's concepts and methods were brought to America and popularized by the Fuller Institute of Church Growth in the early 1980s.

With the publication of Cho's book *Successful Home Cell Groups*, the model took off.[10] It was further propelled by Carl George's Meta Model, a Western adaptation of Cho's principles. It soon became conventional wisdom among church growth leaders and scholars that every large city in America would have a Cho-like church of at least twenty-five thousand to fifty thousand attendees by the end of the century.

Yes, that was by the year 2000.

Whoops!

You can still see Cho's influence in the writings of Dale Galloway, Ralph Neighbour, and a host of other well-respected pundits, some of whom recognize where their core ideas and assumptions come from, while others don't.

I need to acknowledge that some peculiar aspects of Cho's theology have been brought into question, especially in regard to what he calls the "fourth dimension." He's been labeled everything from a heretic to a model of orthodoxy. But since theology is not the subject of this book, I'll leave it to the reader to research and decide whether he has been rightly or unfairly accused. What matters for our purposes is his undeniable impact on the way we do small groups in this country—even in churches that would be quick to decry his theology.

A Nagging Question, a Surprising Answer

Cho's model and concepts were gaining traction at the same time that we at North Coast Church were launching our own model of sermon-based small groups. As I watched the wave of enthusiasm spread, I found myself with some nagging doubts. While I had nothing against Cho or his model (I couldn't argue with its amazing success in Korea and other parts of the world), I had some serious reservations about its adaptability to Western culture and the American church scene.

I remember first sharing my concerns with Lyle Schaller, the brilliant observer of church trends and elder statesmen, back in the late 1980s. I told him that despite all the hype, it didn't seem to me as if this new model was really working anywhere—especially in terms of explosive church growth and evangelism. I asked him if he knew of any places in the United States where it was working as advertised.

I'll never forget his answer.

"I can think of maybe half a dozen."

I was floored. According to my calculations, that equaled six. That was far less than I expected him to say, and if he was right, way out of proportion to the buzz, the conferences, and the books being published.

Looking back, I think he was being generous.

I've since spent a great deal of time studying and reflecting on what went wrong, why a model that works so well in so many parts of the world works so poorly here. I've come to the conclusion that essentially it boils down to three major cultural differences.

A Radically Different View of Christianity

Cho's model is perfectly designed for a culture that has little or no historical connection to evangelical Christianity.

It assumes that non-Christians are best reached through small groups and that healthy small groups will bring people to Christ and into the fellowship of the church. This idea has so permeated the small group movement that some form of Cho's empty chair finds its way into nearly every small group ministry. Sometimes the chair is literal. Sometimes it's not. But there is nearly always a strong belief that the groups can and should be evangelistic.

Yet the reality is that in the American church, very few people come to Christ through a small group. It's much more likely that their first exposure to the gospel will come through a conversation with a friend, followed by a visit to a church's special program or a worship service.

The reason is pretty simple. For the average non-Christian in America, it's far more threatening to walk into a home Bible study than to walk into a worship service. That's because virtually everyone has a vague familiarity with church buildings — even if it's only through an occasional wedding or funeral. They know what the inside looks like. They know they can sit in the back (on the aisle) and quickly leave if things get out of hand.

Not so with a small group that meets in a home or apartment. To most non-Christians, a home Bible study sounds intense, maybe cultish. They have no idea what goes on in there. They wonder, "What if it gets weird? Will people try to sell me something: supplements, indulgences, maybe a time-share? Can I leave if I want to?"

Not sure of the answers, most will politely decline the invitation. It has nothing to do with their preference for worship services over small groups. It has everything to do with their familiarity with one and lack of familiarity with the other.

By way of contrast, in those countries where small groups function as a powerful evangelistic tool, you'll find a cultural context that is exactly the opposite. Christianity is seen as a foreign religion. It has no cultural connect. The average person has no idea what goes on in a worship service. They've never been in a church building. They're hesitant to walk into a worship service — even if invited. It's the temple of a foreign god.

Let me illustrate this principle with a story from my hometown. It's the mirror image of what goes on in South Korea, Africa, Asia, or South America.

I grew up in an area of Southern California known as Hacienda Heights. My parents still live there. For some reason, it's also home to the largest Buddhist temple in the Western hemisphere. Don't ask me why. I have no clue.

Imagine for a moment that my parents were open to Eastern religions (they aren't, but let's pretend). No matter how strong their interest might become, there is no way they'd mosey on down to the Buddhist temple to check it out. They'd be too intimidated. They wouldn't know the protocol, what to do once inside, even how to get inside.

The only way they'd ever find their way into the temple would be by first connecting with some folks who were Buddhist or knowledgeable about Buddhism. Once my parents had a chance to learn about it in a smaller, more social setting, they might, if they felt comfortable enough, agree to go and see what the temple was all about. But it would be a huge step, and they'd never go without first knowing something about the religion and what goes on in there.

The only exception I've found to this principle is in the recovery movement, where small groups seem to be an effective evangelistic side door into the church all across the nation. I think it's because, having hit bottom, these folks have an openness to try anything, including a small group. The concerns that give pause to the average American are overcome by their desperation and desire for sobriety. And once they find sobriety, they often end up finding the Lord as well.

A Radically Different View of Authority

Another major difference between the places where Cho's model leads to explosive growth and the places where it flounders can be found in their radically different views of spiritual authority.

His model works best in cultures that respond well to strong authoritarian leadership. When told to join a cell group, his people sign up. When told to fill the empty chair, they fill it. When asked what happens to those who fail to fill their empty chair, Cho said that he simply tells them that they have sinned against God and their pastor and they need to go to Prayer Mountain to repent.

Now, if you're an American pastor, I dare you to try that line at home. You'll be the one headed to Prayer Mountain.

Whether it's the Ivory Coast, South America, Asia, or the house church movement in China, everywhere you find some version of this model producing explosive growth and evangelism, you'll also find a long history of military coups, tribal chieftains, and dominant male leadership. That's a far cry from the typical Western or European setting, where an emphasis on democracy and the autonomy of the individual permeates everything—including church governance and our models of spiritual leadership.

This is an important distinction, too often missed by those who try to copy or adapt the Korean model. It's a lot easier to get everyone into a small group, to get them to fill an empty chair, and to convince them to grow and divide when they're used to being told what to do—and they actually do it!

A Radically Different Society

A third major cultural distinctive that impacts how well this model will or won't work is the level of mobility within a society and the extent to which people have strong extended-family ties.

Cho's model works best in a society that lacks mobility and therefore produces plenty of long-term relationships and an abundance of extended-family relationships. Again, that greatly impacts the ease with which people both extend and accept an invitation to a small group setting. It's much less inhibiting to go to a home or apartment when you already know some of the people there—or they might even be a distant relative.

In a highly mobile culture like that of the United States, most of our relational ties are weak; they're short-term and role based rather than long-term or family based. When I'm speaking at a conference and ask for a show of hands, it's rare for anyone with grown children to have all their children living within a twenty-five-mile radius. It's even rarer for anyone to have many cousins and distant relatives living nearby. In many cases, they don't even know where their cousins live anymore. And hardly anybody has true lifelong friends and acquaintances.

Contrast that with what happens in a society with low mobility or strong extended-family ties. Relationally, everything changes.

For instance, my wife is an ethnic Armenian. Her grandparents escaped to America during the Armenian genocide, each as the only surviving member of their immediate family. Many Armenians share a similar story or know someone who does. That creates an instant connect when my wife meets another Armenian. They immediately begin the do-you-know-so-and-so dialog. After that they run through the somewhere-in-the-past-we-must-be-related routine. It's as if they assume an immediate level of relationship until or unless it's broken.

If Nancy were to invite any of them to come to a Bible study in our home, most would come at least once.

My experience as a typical member of the American melting pot is quite different. I'm an ethnic mutt. My lineage wanders through New England, Alabama, and Southern California. The only natural connection I assume when I meet someone is a distant relative named Adam. People have to earn my trust—and I have to earn theirs. It's a typical American response. It's what happens when everybody moves all the time.

It makes it much tougher for me to get a new friend or stranger to come to a Bible study at my home. So we end up with a house full of Armenians.

When taken together, these significant cultural differences add up. They help to explain why Cho's model (and most of the current adaptations of his model) didn't work very well in your church—or mine, for that matter.

It's not that it's a bad model. It's an incredible model. It's just not a very good cultural fit for most American churches.

Prayer Mountain

Prayer Mountain was established by Cho's church in 1973. Set aside as a special place to seek God, it can accommodate nearly ten thousand people at once. It has a large number of small cubicles where prayer warriors can lock themselves away for extended prayer and fasting.

Needless to say, American pastors who've traveled to Korea are blown away. Many come back wondering why Koreans have such a passion for prayer and what they can do to ignite it in the American church.

While the Korean church may well have a deeper hunger for God and a better understanding of the importance of prayer, it also has a cultural predisposition to go to Prayer Mountain when told to do so.

In contrast, the Western church has the opposite cultural predisposition. We ignore and even rebel against strong authoritarian styles of leadership. We don't like to be told what to do.

I don't know. But something tells me this is a difference that needs to be accounted for before we make blanket judgments.

Chapter 19

Before You Start

Five Key Questions

One of the biggest mistakes leaders make when it comes to either launching or reengineering a small group ministry is a failure to carefully align both vision and methods. The result is often a ministry that functions much like an automobile with its front tires badly out of alignment. While it can still get down the road, the ride is way too bumpy and the tires wear out way too quickly.

That's why I always encourage pastors and church leaders to work through a series of five key "alignment" questions *before* launching or reengineering their small group ministry. After the fact, these questions are nowhere near as powerful. Because even though they point out what's wrong and why things aren't working well, it's tough to make the changes the answers call for once a ministry has already been launched.

Churches tend to treat their existing small group ministries a lot like many of us treat our cars. Just because it starts to pull to one side or the other doesn't mean we do anything. Instead, we wait until it starts to shake like a fat guy at the prom. Then we take it in for an alignment. In the same way, as long as a ministry is still limping along, few churches are willing to make significant changes. The price is too high, and the benefits are hard to see ahead of time.

I've used the following five questions with church planters, seasoned pastors, small churches, and megachurches. The results are always the same. When carefully worked through, they will practically guarantee a small group ministry that performs well, one that not only aligns vision and methods but also fits the underlying philosophy of discipleship, the unique cultural context, and the ministry DNA of the church. Here they are.

Who Are You Trying to Reach?

The first question I ask is, "Who are you trying to reach?" By that I mean, "Specifically who do you imagine being in your small groups? Who is likely to opt out? Who are you willing to leave out?"

Too often the initial answer is, "We want everyone to be in a group."

But not everyone will be in a group. It'll never happen. Based on how your groups are organized and what you do in them, some people will come and some won't. Aiming at everyone guarantees that you have targeted no one.

Every programmatic decision we make loses someone and draws someone else. That's why a big part of deciding who we'll reach is choosing—ahead of time—who we're willing to lose.

To identify the different options, imagine a funnel that starts with everyone at the top. Below, in a narrower part of the funnel, is a smaller subset made up of all those who have an interest in spiritual things. Farther down are those who go beyond spiritual interest to actively seeking God. Next are those who actually turn to Christ, followed by those who take their spiritual growth seriously. Toward the bottom you'll find a still smaller group of folks who might be described as being on fire for God, ready to charge hell with a water pistol. Finally, popping out at the bottom is the smallest group yet: leaders.

The funnel looks something like this:

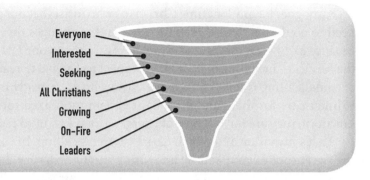

Everyone
Interested
Seeking
All Christians
Growing
On-Fire
Leaders

After explaining this funnel, I always ask pastors and church leaders, "Which of these groups do you *want* to reach the most?"

Notice that I don't ask, "Which group *should* you want to reach the most?" That only tells me their level of political correctness.

I often have to push back a little here to be sure I'm getting a heartfelt vision rather than one that's driven by political correctness. I've learned that people whose hearts are bent toward raising up high-impact leaders sometimes tell me they're committed to reaching seekers. They don't want to sound like they're cold to the Great Commission. Meanwhile others with great gifts and passion for evangelism tell me they're all about discipleship and growing people deeper.

My bias is that no particular emphasis is more God-pleasing than another. While the larger body of Christ must be focused on the entire spectrum of people, no one individual or single church is called or gifted to reach everyone or do everything. It's neither possible nor biblical.

For instance, at North Coast my personal vision has always been that *every Christian* in our church needs to be velcroed to significant relationships. I see it as the way spiritual growth best happens and the most powerful way to make our church sticky.

Right or wrong, that's my paradigm.

It explains why I don't mind when those who are merely spiritually interested find our groups to be too demanding or when most seekers wait until they've stepped over the line to follow Jesus before joining one of our groups.

Same goes for any longtime Christians who insist that our groups need to go deeper. It's easy for me to resist the changes they want, because to do what they want would drive away everyone farther up the funnel — including many of the people I feel called to reach. My personal calling is not primarily to those who are already mature. While I care for them and want to see them mobilized for God's kingdom, they are but a subset of a larger group I want to reach.

That's my vision and North Coast Church's calling. In contrast, the sweet spot of your calling and vision might be a very different place on the funnel. What's important is that your leadership team is in agreement as to who you most want to be in your small groups. Until you've figured that out, it's pretty hard to design a ministry to reach them.

What Are You Planning to Do?

The second question I ask is, "What do you plan to do in your meetings?" The options are endless. But once I know what happens in a small group, I can predict with uncanny accuracy who will come and who won't.

I've noticed that many pastors and leaders start with what they want to see happen in a small group rather than who they hope to reach. The result is often a well-designed program with a fancy leader's manual that describes a romantic image of how an ideal small group should function, but the program has absolutely no appeal to or stickiness with the people it's supposed to reach.

For instance, one pastor told me how pumped up he was about the new small group program his church was launching. It was going to take the entire church to a new level of discipleship. Along with the weekly study, everyone would be committed to memorizing Scriptures and holding one another accountable to share their faith with at least one non-Christian every week.

I remember being impressed and thinking what a great impact it would have on the group members and on his church as a whole.

That is, until I heard him also say that he'd given the new pastor in charge of small groups a mandate to get 50 percent of the congregation into a group by the end of the year.

My next thought was that his small group pastor had better polish up his resume—fast. There was no way he'd ever be able to reach that goal.

The pastor's plan was designed for people way down the funnel. It would intimidate anyone new in the faith. It would scare off everyone who lacked the time or motivation to memorize large chunks of Scripture. It would freak out anyone too shy to talk to strangers on a weekly basis.

It's not that what he wanted to do couldn't work or wouldn't have a positive impact on his church. It could and it would, but not with 50 percent of his congregation. Fifteen to 20 percent, maybe; 50 percent, no way!

What my pastor friend didn't understand was that every time we raise the bar of what we expect from and do in a small group, we proportionally shrink the number of people who will be in a small group. That's not a call to lower expectations. It is a recognition of the funnel principle. It's a call to carefully think through the impact of what we choose to do in a group ahead of time and to decide if it helps or hinders us in reaching the people we've been called to reach.

Just as I use a funnel to illustrate the ever-smaller percentage of people who will make their way from spiritually interested to spiritual leadership, so too a funnel can be used to illustrate what happens as we raise the bar of expectations. The activity funnel looks like this:

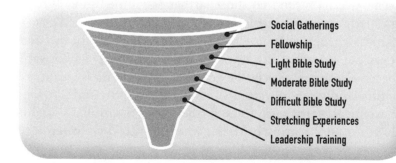

Social Gatherings
Fellowship
Light Bible Study
Moderate Bible Study
Difficult Bible Study
Stretching Experiences
Leadership Training

How Well Do These Match?

The third key alignment question is, "How well does *who* you want to reach match up with *what* you plan to do?" Putting the two funnels together and comparing who we want to reach with what we plan to do can be an eye-opener.

I've used this simple exercise countless times to show pastors and leaders why their groups are or aren't working. The most important thing to understand about any potential misalignment is that what we do will always trump who we want to reach. It's what draws or repels people. We always end up reaching the people who best fit what we choose to do.

Here's how the two funnels match up.

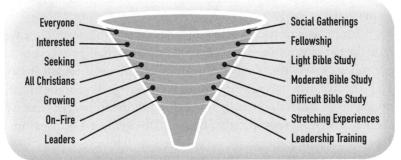

Everyone	Social Gatherings
Interested	Fellowship
Seeking	Light Bible Study
All Christians	Moderate Bible Study
Growing	Difficult Bible Study
On-Fire	Stretching Experiences
Leaders	Leadership Training

Using these funnels, it's easy to understand why North Coast's sermon-based small groups are built around moderate Bible study and application. It's the best way to reach our target audience.

That doesn't mean that those farther down the funnel (growing Christians, on-fire zealots, and leaders) are ignored. We have all kinds of people who have made their way down the funnel and popped out as leaders. But it mostly happens as they step forward to become an apprentice, host a group, or lead. The messy reality of frontline ministry motivates them into deeper study and provides the experiences that push them farther down the funnel—and it does so without scaring off those who are still stuck toward the top.

Now, your focus might be completely different. What's important is that whatever you do matches well with whoever you're called to reach. Otherwise, what you do will, by default, determine who you reach.

What Is Your Philosophy of Discipleship and Leadership Training?

The fourth key question is, "How do you think people are best trained to live out the Christian life and best prepared for leadership?" Your answer should ideally be reflected in the curriculum you choose, the way you structure your meetings, and the way you train your leaders.

I find three basic approaches to discipleship and leadership training in the Christian community. Each has its strengths and weaknesses. Each works better in some settings than in others.

Mentoring

The mentoring model for discipleship and leadership training is primarily focused on one-on-one relationships. It envisions every Christian having a mentor and mentoring someone else down the line.

It's an intense model. At its best, it gives those who are being mentored incredibly customized spiritual support and training.

Its downside is that it's relatively inefficient. It works best in smaller settings. It's easily derailed. The one-on-one orientation makes it vulnerable to the weakest links in the chain. If a few links break, you'll have to scramble to get everything put back together. But its strong emphasis on individual relationships means you might not know a link has broken until long after the fact.

Mentoring seems to work best in situations where the focus is on high commitment and developing high-capacity leaders. Introverts and highly structured individuals often thrive under it. It doesn't do so well in a fast-growing situation or with those who lack a high degree of intrinsic motivation.

Education

In contrast, an educational approach is heavily front-loaded. It expects people to work through a curriculum or set of experiences to be certified as spiritually mature or ready for leadership.

Theological institutions are mostly built on this model. If someone feels called to ministry, they go to a Bible school or a theological seminary to become grounded and learn their craft before launching out. Upon graduation, they're stamped as ready to go. In a church setting, the educational model tends toward a set of core classes, experiences, and workshops that everyone is supposed to go through. Again, once they've finished, they're considered discipled or ready to lead.

It's a comprehensive model. Done well, it covers all the basics and more.

Its major downside is that it takes a long time from start to finish. In a highly mobile culture, lots of people won't be around long enough to complete the process. In high-growth situations, it's hard to ever have enough leaders who've graduated.

It also tends to work best with linear and goal-oriented personalities. It's not so good with those who are entrepreneurial, artsy, have a trace of ADD, or simply don't like jumping through hoops.

Apprenticeship

The apprenticeship model tends to throw people into a task and then come alongside to help as needed.

It's similar to what I experienced while working as a grocery clerk during my college years. One day I was told that I was being transferred and promoted to the produce department. That was fine, except I hardly knew the difference between a watermelon and a tomato.

That didn't seem to bother management. They saw me as a good worker. They figured that as long as there was a well-trained produce manager nearby, I could learn on the job, without doing too much damage along the way.

They were right. I made lots of mistakes. But most of them were small and inconsequential. All of them were made with a skilled journeyman nearby who stopped me or helped to pick up the pieces.

The upside of the apprenticeship model is that it gets lots of people into the game quickly. In a fast-growing situation, it's often the only way to produce enough leaders; the same goes for highly mobile situations. It works well with those who flourish in less structured environments and accommodates the meandering path to spiritual growth that most people take.

Its downside is that it often puts people into leadership before they're ready. While that is an intentional part of the model, if there isn't a journeyman around to help or pick up the pieces when needed, it can create quite a mess before anybody notices.

All of these models can work. But whichever one best fits the DNA of your church and the unique situation you minister in should be the model you use for discipleship and leadership training. If not, the lack of alignment between your small group structures and how you think people grow and leaders develop will create some serious bumps, eventually causing the groups to fall apart.

Who Can We Speed Model?

The final question to ask before launching a new or revamped small group ministry is, "Who already does what we want to do well—*and does it in a church we would go to if we lived in the area?*"

The typical pattern when starting up or revamping a small group ministry is to search for what businesses call "best practices." We try to find out who is doing it best.

But that can be a big mistake.

The reason is that just because a church does small groups well doesn't mean they're doing something that will work in your church. As we saw with Cho's small groups, a model ideally suited for one situation can be a complete misfit for another. The best way to make sure a model is transferable to your situation is to ask yourself whether you would go to that church if you lived in that town.

If the answer is no, odds are that what they are doing won't work where you are ministering.

It reminds me of what I used to call the Willow Creek effect. Many pastors benefited greatly and came home energized and equipped to expand their ministry after a conference at Willow Creek Church. But others had a completely different experience. They came home and nearly tore their church apart.

It wasn't Willow's fault. It was the returning pastors' fault.

More than a few have gone to one of these conferences and seen the food court, the huge crowds, and lots of new Christians, and said, "That's what I want and need." But in the next breath, I'd hear them criticize the lack of participatory worship, the absence of verse-by-verse expository preaching, and a host of other things. In other words, if they lived in Barrington, Illinois, they wouldn't go to Willow Creek. No wonder the insights and strategies didn't work back home. They weren't a cultural fit.

It's much wiser to find a model that works well (even if it's not the best model out there) in a church you and most of your people would attend. That almost always guarantees a strong fit with the DNA and culture of your church.

Sticky churches are ultimately held together by strong webs of relationships. That's why a healthy and highly attended small group ministry can slam the back door shut. But alignment is essential. Without it, things will bump along. People will burn out. With it, things will hum along and people will stick around for a long, long time.

Acknowledgments

To Mike Yearley, Charlie Bradshaw, Chris Mavity, Dave Enns, and Ned Mervich, special thanks for the incredible leadership you've brought to the growth group ministry at North Coast Church. Each of you has put your own lasting stamp on the ministry and left a powerful legacy for those who will follow. Without your wisdom, hard work, and commitment, sermon-based small groups would be nothing more than an idealistic idea. You've made that idea into the powerful reality it is now.

To my wife, Nancy, thank you for your wise advice, always kind way of delivering it, and careful proofing. To Cheryl Downing, Kathie Duncan, and Erica Ramos, thank you for your insights and much-needed corrections of my sometimes creative spelling and occasionally convoluted grammar.

To Charlie, Chris Brown, and Paul Savona, thanks for making ministry such a delight and for taking North Coast to heights I never could have taken it to alone. To the Elder Board at North Coast, your wise counsel, constant encouragement, and willingness to take a risk have made ministry a blast.

To my parents, Bill and Carolyn Osborne, thanks for the privilege of being raised in a home that is both Christian and functional, qualities that are all too rare these days. You laid the foundation for whatever wisdom and leadership I've been able to offer the body of Christ. The stupid ideas and decisions are all mine.

Writing Great Questions

North Coast Church's Sermon-Based Small Group Question Writing Template

Every set of weekly study questions should incorporate each of the following three kinds of questions. However, it *is not* necessary or advisable to always ask them in order.

1. *Getting to Know Me.* These are history-giving questions designed to surface answers that are self-revealing and informative. The questions should be nonthreatening and safe. They should speed up the process of developing a shared history.

2. *Into the Bible.* These are questions that draw group members into the Bible to discover truth from passages that were not the primary text for the weekend message. They may be explanatory or in some way shed further light on the main topic or principles of the sermon. They should offer a sense of "something more."

3. *Application.* These are questions based directly on the application points of the weekend message. They should ask participants to examine their lives in light of the primary truth(s) taught or explored in the sermon. Application questions do not have to regurgitate every take-home point of the message. They can focus on one, some, or all of the main points.

Getting-to-Know-Me Questions
For the First Few Weeks of a New Group

1. What section of the newspaper do you read first—funnies, sports, world news, local news, editorial, business? Why?

2. What vacation or big trip (either as a child or as an adult) did you enjoy the most?

3. When you are lost, which of the following are you most likely to do?
   a. stop and ask for directions
   b. check a map
   c. drive around until you find the place you're looking for
   d. not admit to anyone that you're lost
4. When you undress at night, do you tend to put your clothes on a hanger, fold them over a chair, stuff them into a hamper, or leave them on the floor? Be honest!

For Established Groups

After a few weeks, history-giving questions can come right out of the sermon or biblical text. While tied to the message, they still need to be safe and nonthreatening. Some examples:

1. (for a message on the miracle of Lazarus): What is the most amazing thing you've ever seen?
2. (for a message on the Prodigal Son): Which of the following characters in the story do you most identify with—and why?
   a. the father
   b. the rebel son
   c. the "good" brother
   d. the friends at the party
   e. another character: _____
3. (for a message on Matthew 7:1–5): Which phrase(s) best describe(s) the attitudes in the home you grew up in—and why?
   a. high expectations
   b. live and let live
   c. harsh
   d. tolerant
   e. merciful

Into-the-Bible Questions

These questions come from passages not explicitly covered in the sermon. They create a sense of digging deeper. They can be everything from Old Testament case studies illustrating a main point or principle to parallel passages. They can deal with all of the points and topics from the message, or they can zero in on just one point or topic. It should take anywhere from fifteen to thirty minutes to look up the verses and answer all of these questions. Here are some samples from actual sermons (with the sermon title listed first).

How a Crowd Becomes a Church

It's easy to get sidetracked. Even the early church had trouble staying devoted to the right things. Read the following passages in Revelation. They describe Jesus' perspective on some of the first-century churches. Jot down what they were doing right and where they got off track. (Five passages from Revelation 2 – 3 were listed, with two blank columns labeled "What They Did Right" and "What They Did Wrong.")

A Short Course on Miracles

As we saw in this weekend's message, God's miracles are completely unpredictable. While we know that our God is always good and powerful, he doesn't always do what we expect. Here are some other messy situations from the book of Acts. Read each one and jot down how God responded. (Four passages from Acts were listed.)

What insights into God's power and our response during a difficult situation can you draw from these passages? Put your answers in your own words.

How the Wise Gain Wealth

When it comes to money, a proper attitude and perspective is vital. Each of the following Scriptures speaks of an attitude we need to have or avoid when it comes to money. Read each one and then jot down in your own words what it says. (A total of nine passages from both the Old and New Testaments were listed.)

Which one of these attitudes comes easiest to you?

Which ones have you most struggled with in the past?

Application Questions

These questions should relate to the main points and applications from the sermon. They may deal with all of them or just one particularly important point or principle. These sermon application questions may be couched in a variety of formats. Here are some examples — once again showing actual questions used in past homework.

Priming the Pump

These questions are open-ended. They allow a leader to quickly gauge which issues or points are most relevant. Here are some examples.

1. As you reflect on last weekend's sermon, what one principle or insight stands out as being particularly helpful, insightful, or difficult to grasp?
2. If Pastor Larry had to give an abbreviated version of last weekend's message, what two points or ideas would you tell him to include no matter what?
3. What's one thing from last weekend's sermon that you hope we talk about as a group?
4. Was there any one thing that you most agreed with or disagreed with from last weekend's message? What was it and why?

Connecting

These questions help people connect their personal life experiences to the topic on hand, and they give those who are willing a chance to share.

1. *A Short Course on Miracles.* This week we saw that no matter what God does, when someone doesn't want to believe, they won't believe. Have you ever seen this occur? What happened?
2. *Matthew 7:1 – 5.* This weekend we contrasted the biblical concept of tolerance with our culture's definition of the term. How do the major differences between the two impact the following situations?
   a. You have a coworker who asks you about your church or your faith.
   b. A neighbor asks you what you think of a high-profile religious leader who has recently been in the news for a moral failure.
   c. A friend walks out of a long-term but tough marriage. Your other friends say you have no right to judge.

How do you think our culture's high value on religious tolerance has impacted your own approach to other faiths and Christ?

3. *The Dangerous Side of Wealth.* Pastor Larry pointed out four dumb things we can do with our money: hoard it; fail to pay what we owe; enjoy luxury without generosity; use it to crush others.
   a. Which of these do you think is the most common among fellow Christians?
   b. What do you think is the biggest issue for non-Christians?
   c. Which do you struggle with most? Least?

Digging Deeper

These questions are designed to be self-revealing. Leaders are instructed to handle them with wisdom and tact. No one should ever be pressured to share their answers to a digging-deeper question — though experience shows that most people will be willing to share their answers as the group grows more tightly knit. Here are some examples.

1. *Staying on Track.* Looking back on your own spiritual journey, have there been some specific areas where you have a tendency to get off track in your walk with God? If so, what helps you get back on track?
2. *Telling Your Story.* Is anything keeping you from effectively sharing Jesus Christ with others? Are there any adjustments you need to make in either your message or your attitudes? If so, what would it take?
3. *Hanging On.* Trials can be especially difficult when we try to face them alone. Who are some of the people in your life you can depend on to hear you and pray with you during a difficult time? Is there anything you are going through right now that your growth group could be praying for and helping you with, if they only knew about it?

Appendix 2

Sample Sermon Note Sheet and Study Questions

Following are samples of the weekend note sheet and the growth group homework sheet that are placed inside the weekly bulletin. Also included is a sample of the note sheet with the answers filled in.

The Jesus Story: 33 Years That Changed the World North Coast Church
Luke 15:11–32: Message #10 Date

A Different Kind of Love
Luke 15:11–32

The Well-Known Story
A Father and His Wayward Son

Setting the Context
Luke 15:1–3

Religious leaders were upset that Jesus _____ rather than _____ people of questionable character.

The Main Point
Luke 15:11–32/ Matthew 9:10–13/ 2 Peter 3:7–9

God would rather _____ than _____ .

How to Love and Respond to a Rebel
Lessons from a Prodigal's Father

1. **When They Insist On Leaving,** _____ !
Luke 15:11–13 & 24, 32

   Two BIG mistakes. . .
   Raising the _____ .
   Matthew 11:28–30 & 1 John 5:3/ Ephesians 6:4 & Colossians 3:21
   Sticking our _____ .
   Galatians 6:7–8/ 1 Samuel 2:1–3:18 (see 3:13)/ Proverbs 20:11 & 26

2. **When Things Get Tough,** _____ .
Luke 15:13–19/ Judges 10:10–16/ Isaiah 1:13–20

   If we soften the _____ , we'll lengthen the _____ .

3. **When They Come Back,** _____ .
Luke 15:20–24/ Luke 15:1–10/ Romans 5:8

4. **After They're Back,** _____ !
Luke 15:28–32 (see 15:31)/ 2 Samuel 12:7–14 (see 12:13–14)/ Jeremiah 18:1–8

   Don't confuse restoring the _____ with removing all the _____ .

Growth Group Homework

For the Week of _____

Getting Started

1. What insight, principle, or observation from this weekend's message did you find to be most helpful, eye-opening, or troubling? Explain.

2. Most of us have a bias toward being either a *bleeding heart* or a *strict disciplinarian.*
   a. Which one most characterized the home you grew up in?

   b. Which do you tend toward in your relationships with others?

3. If you had to identify with just one of the three individuals in this parable (the father, the young prodigal, or the older brother), who would it be and why?

4. In the Old Testament, the nation of Israel was infamous for rebelling against God's leadership. This week, we'll study a couple of passages that show how God responded when they acted like a prodigal. As you read, notice the points where God's response parallels the principles from Luke 15.
    - *If a rebel insists on leaving—let them leave.*
    - *When things get tough—let them hit bottom.*
    - *When they come back—run to greet them.*
    - *After they're back—don't punish the obedient.*

    a. Read Psalm 78:54–64. Jot down any insights, questions, or key observations.

    b. Read Psalm 106:32–48. Jot down any insights, questions, or key observations.

5. Have you ever learned a valuable lesson because of a failure (big or small) that God or someone else stepped back and allowed you to experience? If so, and you're comfortable sharing it, share the failure and what you learned.

6. Imagine for a moment that you were the rebellious son in the parable we studied this week. How do you think you would have felt when you saw your father running to meet you on your way home?

7. Do you agree with the following statement? "The older brother in this parable responded appropriately in light of what he knew at the time."

Explain your answer.

Digging Deeper

8. When faced with a prodigal in your life (assuming that the prodigal son can represent a family member, a friend, a coworker, or a social outcast), which of the four principles for loving and responding to a rebel do you come by most naturally?

    a. Which comes hardest?

    b. Is there anything you need to do as a result of what you've learned this week?

A Different Kind of Love
Luke 15:11–32

The Well-Known Story
A Father and His Wayward Son

Setting the Context
Luke 15:1–3

Religious leaders were upset that Jesus _____**welcomed**_____ rather than _____**excluded**_____ people of questionable character.

The Main Point
Luke 15:11–32/ Matthew 9:10–13/ 2 Peter 3:7–9

God would rather _____**restore**_____ than _____**punish**_____ .

How to Love and Respond to a Rebel
Lessons from a Prodigal's Father

1. When They Insist On Leaving, _____**Let Them Leave**_____ !
Luke 15:11–13 & 24, 32

Two BIG mistakes...

Raising the _____**bar too high**_____ .
Matthew 11:28–30 & 1 John 5:3/ Ephesians 6:4 & Colossians 3:21

Sticking our _____**head in the sand**_____ .
Galatians 6:7–8/ 1 Samuel 2:1–3:18 (see 3:13)/ Proverbs 20:11 & 26

2. When Things Get Tough, _____**Let Them Hit Bottom**_____ .
Luke 15:13–19/ Judges 10:10–16/ Isaiah 1:13–20

If we soften the _____**blows**_____ , we'll lengthen the _____**rebellion**_____ .

3. When They Come Back, _____**Run to Greet Them**_____ .
Luke 15:20–24/ Luke 15:1–10/ Romans 5:8

4. After They're Back, _____**Don't Punish the Obedient**_____ !
Luke 15:28–32 (see 15:31)/ 2 Samuel 12:7–14 (see 12:13–14)/ Jeremiah 18:1–8

Don't confuse restoring the _____**Relationship**_____ with removing all the _____**Consequences**_____ .

Sample Growth Group Covenant

This covenant is reviewed and signed at the beginning of each quarter by all groups. Groups that are continuing still review the covenant during the first meeting of each quarter.

Session Dates _____ to _____ .
Leader(s) _____ Phone # _____ .
Host(s) _____ Phone # _____ .

This covenant will help us discuss and clarify our goals, expectations, and commitments as a group. Since healthy groups thrive on trust and participation, a clear covenant is an important starting point toward a successful group experience.

Growth Groups: Our Basic Purpose

Growth groups exist to promote the development of significant Christian relationships centered around the study of God's Word (see Hebrews 10:24–25; Romans 8:29).

Sharing

Each week, we will take time to share what is happening in our lives. At first this sharing will include some planned "sharing questions." After the first few weeks, it will become more informal and personal as our group feels safer and more comfortable.

Study

Each week we'll study a portion of God's Word that relates to the previous weekend's sermon. Our goal is to learn how to apply and live out our Christianity in our day-to-day experiences and relationships.

Support

Each week, we'll learn how to take care of one another as Christ commanded (see John 15:9–13). This care will take many forms, such as praying, listening, meeting needs, and encouraging and even challenging one another as needed.

Five Marks of a Healthy Group

For our group to be healthy, we need to

1. focus on spiritual growth as a top priority (Romans 8:29);
2. accept one another in love just as Christ has accepted us (Romans 15:7);
3. take care of one another in love without crossing over the line into parenting or taking inappropriate responsibility for solving the problems of others (John 13:34);
4. treat one another with respect in both speech and action (Ephesians 4:25 – 5:2);
5. keep our commitments to the group — including attending regularly, doing the homework, and keeping confidences whenever requested (Psalm 15:1 – 2, 4b).

Guidelines and Covenant

1. Dates   We'll meet on _____ nights for _____ weeks.
Our final meeting of the quarter will be on _____.

2. Time   We'll arrive between _____ and _____ and begin the meeting at _____ .
We'll spend approximately _____ minutes in singing (optional), _____ minutes in study/discussion, and _____ minutes in prayer/sharing.

3. Children   Group members are responsible to arrange childcare for their children. Nursing newborns are welcome, provided they are not a distraction to the group.

4. Study   Each week, we'll study the same topic(s) covered in the previous weekend's sermon.

5. Prayer   Our group will be praying each week for one another and specific missions requests.

6. Homework and Attendance

> Joining a growth group requires a commitment *to attend each week and to do the homework ahead of time.* Obviously, allowances are made for sickness, vacation, work conflicts, and other special events—but not much more! *This commitment is the key to a healthy group.*

> Most weeks, the homework will require from twenty to thirty minutes to adequately prepare for the group study and discussion.

> If we cannot come to a meeting, we will _____
> _____ .

7. Refreshments

8. Social(s)

9. Service Project(s)

We agree together in Christ to honor this covenant.
(To be decided on and signed by each group member on or before the third week.)

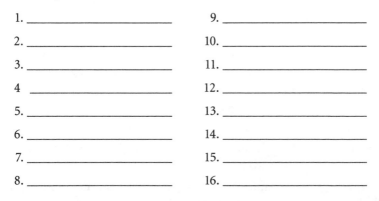

1. _____   9. _____
2. _____   10. _____
3. _____   11. _____
4 _____   12. _____
5. _____   13. _____
6. _____   14. _____
7. _____   15. _____
8. _____   16. _____

End-of-the-Quarter Evaluation Form

This form is filled out by all group members at the end of each ten- to eleven-week small group session. Notice that it gives those who are not continuing an easy off-ramp.

Group Name: _____

Your Name: _____

One of the best ways to improve any group is to evaluate it! Tonight you have the opportunity to assess both the strengths and the weaknesses of your particular group. The questions below will help you think through different aspects of your group life. Please answer them *thoroughly* and *honestly*.

The Group

One of the things I've enjoyed most about being in the group this quarter is:

Are you happy with the amout of time we spend each week in:	Yes	No	Comments
Discussion			
Study			
Prayer			
Worship (if applicable)			

Is the length of the meeting appropriate? Yes _____ No _____
Please explain.

How have the group discussions gone? Is everyone who wants to share able to share? Are there any people or issues that quell the discussion? Explain:

Do you have any suggestions for improving the meetings?

My Plans

For the next growth group session, I'm planning to

1. remain in the same growth group.
2. try a new growth group.
3. take a break from growth groups.

Homework

What do you like most about the homework?

What do you like the least?

If you could change just one thing about the homework, what would it be and why?

The amount of homework is

    1. just about right.
    2. a little too much.
    3. not quite enough. *Please explain.*

My Leader

One of the things I appreciate most about my small group leader is:

If your leader asked for advice on whether he or she should talk *more, less,* or *exactly the same* during your meetings, what would you say?

Is there anything your leader could do to make your meetings even better?

My Host

One of the things I appreciate most about our host is:

Is there anything your host could do to make your meetings better? (Seating arrangements, lighting, temperature, refreshments, socials, etc.)

Leader Training Topics

This is not an exhaustive list. It is given to prime the pump and help you discover the topics that will best fit your ministry situation.

Potential Rookie Training Topics (for New Leaders)

1. Learning to Listen
2. The Art of Asking (How to Ask Good Questions)
3. How to Run a Meeting (Preparation, Flexibility, Tangents, and Transitions)
4. Group Prayer (Helping Your Quieter Members Learn to Pray)
5. Study Tools (Tools to Help You Better Prepare for Your Study)
6. Proactive Leadership (Becoming a Problem Solver, Going After Problems Proactively, Taking Responsibility)
7. Dealing with a Loudmouth and Other EGRs (Extra-Grace-Required People)
8. Flock- or Lamb-Focused (How to Keep One Sick Lamb from Destroying the Entire Flock)

Potential Veteran Training Topics (for Continuing Leaders)

1. Summer Sabbath
2. Motivation: Push, Pull, or Plead?
3. No One Walks Alone (Active Listening and Knowing When to Butt In and When to Butt Out)
4. Spiritual Gifts (Tools and Inventories)
5. Life Mapping
6. Balance (Covey's Four Quadrants)
7. How to Have a Great Service Project
8. Study Tools (Tools to Help You Better Prepare for Your Study)
9. The Silence of Adam (Book Review)
10. Connecting (Book Review)

11. When All Hell Breaks Loose (Handling a Major Crisis in Your Group)
12. Emotional Intelligence
13. Visiting the Hospital (Tips for Responding to Illness, Loss, and Even Death in Your Group)
14. How to Handle a Crusader (Dealing with a Single-Issue Zealot)

Leader Responsibilities

This is a list of the responsibilities that are presented to leaders *before* they agree to lead.

Leaders are expected to do the following:

Prepare and Lead the Meeting

Along with listening to the sermon and completing the weekly homework, leaders also need to listen to the weekly *Leader's Training*. This short audio can be accessed on the Web or played from a CD we will provide you with every week. It will give you helpful tips for leading your small group as well as keep you abreast of upcoming events. It is designed to share with you *insider information* appropriate for key leaders within our ministry.

Attend All Training Meetings

For new leaders and hosts we have an all-day "Rookie Training" at the church. This is for both husbands and wives. This year's training will be held on _____.

For all leaders and hosts our annual Leader/Host Kickoff is held in September. This year's kickoff will be held at the church on

_____.

Ongoing leadership training is provided throughout the year for both rookie and veteran leaders on a periodic basis. Sometimes the training is held in a large group setting at the church. Other times it will be a smaller-cluster meeting in a home.

Track the Needs of Group Members

As a group leader, you will often be the first line of spiritual defense in the lives of your group members. It will be your responsibility (along with your host) to keep in touch with the spiritual pulse of the people in your group.

Communicate Special Needs Up-Line to Your Coach and/or Pastors

It's possible that some issues will surface in your group or in a member's life that are beyond your experience, expertise, or comfort zone. In that case, communicate your concerns up-line to either your coach or one of the pastors on staff for guidance or additional help.

Complete Weekly Attendance Sheets

Group leaders need to turn in a weekly attendance sheet. This can be done online. These attendance sheets are very important. They not only help us track who is in a group; they also help the pastoral staff keep an overall pulse on the groups as a whole.

Visit Members in the Hospital

When a crisis or major illness hits, your group needs to spring into action. While your host will take the lead in providing any needed meals or practical help, you as a small group leader need to be sure that you and others from the group are available for prayer and support.

Host Responsibilities

This is a list of the responsibilities that are presented to hosts *before* they agree to host.

As a growth group host, you do much more than just provide a home or apartment to meet in! You are a vital part of the leadership team. The combination of a committed leader and a committed host (each focusing on their role within the group) is hard to beat. Here's a list of some of your primary responsibilities. Hosts are expected to do the following:

Provide a Clean, Comfortable Home Environment

Some key questions:

Is my house clean and picked up by meeting time? A clean living room, kitchen, and bathroom help people relax and feel comfortable.

Do I have enough comfortable chairs? Hard chairs make for a long meeting! If needed, you can purchase padded folding chairs for a nominal price at a local store.

Do I have enough lighting? A well-lit (not glaring!) room energizes a group, while a dark or dimly room de-energizes it. Maybe it's time to add a lamp to that dark corner!

Is my house free of dog or cat odors? If you have indoor pets, your house may well have odors that you've grown used to. Ask a good friend for an honest evaluation! Also, remember that many people are allergic to dogs or cats. It's a good idea to ask your group about this at your first meeting. If it's a problem, you may need to keep your animals out of the house before or during the meeting.

Are my children interrupting the group? It's important that children do not interrupt the flow of the meeting, either by coming into the room or by requiring you to leave the meeting. Of course, there will be times when this is unavoidable due to an emergency or special circumstance. But such times should be the exception, not the rule. If children are interrupting or within earshot, the honesty and transparency of the group will suffer.

Provide a Warm and Friendly Environment

This involves things like introducing folks to one another during your first potluck/meeting; making sure to talk with and involve the shy or quiet members before and after meetings; and keeping in touch with group members between meetings.

Provide Feedback for the Leader

One of the host's most important jobs is to discuss and evaluate the group with the leader on a regular basis. This often can be done informally after everyone leaves. Items to discuss include the following: What's going well in the group? What's not? Who's hurting? How can you, as a host, help? Is the meeting moving along at a good pace? Is it dragging at some points?

Provide Support for the Leader

Another way to help your leader is to jump-start the discussion when it lags. Sometimes a question will elicit no response (either because everyone is nervous or because the question is unclear). Whenever this happens, you can assist your leader by breaking the ice and answering the question yourself. Or, if the question is unclear, you can ask the leader to rephrase it. This provides an opportunity to regroup and come at the issue from a different angle. Knowing that a host will help him or her out of a jam gives a leader a lot of security.

Organize Meals for Members in the Hospital or Meet Other Special Needs

One of a host's most important jobs is to make sure that anyone in the group who faces a significant crisis gets the practical help and support they need. Hosts should organize the group to meet practical needs, provide meals, or render any special assistance that's needed.

Organize Refreshments, Socials, and Service Projects

Refreshments. Hosts are responsible to organize the weekly refreshments and/or desserts. The host is *not* expected to provide them.

Quarterly socials. With the help of the group, the host makes sure there is at least one social event during the quarter.

Service projects. With the help of the leader, each group needs to carry out two service projects during the year. The Community Service ministry will help you choose and coordinate a service project, unless you have one that you or your group are already connected with.

Appendix 8

A List of New Testament "One Anothers"

This is a list of the things Christians are commanded to do with and for one another. It's a list of commands that are hard to fulfill in a large group setting. They are best fulfilled within the framework of close and accountable relationships similar to those found in a healthy small group.

Love one another.

John 13:34–35: "A new command I give you: Love one another. As I have loved you, so you must love one another. By this all men will know that you are my disciples, if you love one another."

John 15:12–13: "My command is this: Love each other as I have loved you. Greater love has no one than this, that he lay down his life for his friends."

John 15:17: "This is my command: Love each other."

Romans 13:8: "Let no debt remain outstanding, except the continuing debt to love one another, for he who loves his fellowman has fulfilled the law."

1 Thessalonians 4:9: "Now about brotherly love we do not need to write to you, for you yourselves have been taught by God to love each other."

Hebrews 13:1: "Keep on loving each other as brothers."

1 Peter 1:22: "Now that you have purified yourselves by obeying the truth so that you have sincere love for your brothers, love one another deeply, from the heart."

1 Peter 4:8: "Above all, love each other deeply, because love covers over a multitude of sins."

1 John 3:11: "This is the message you heard from the beginning: We should love one another."

1 John 3:23: "This is his command: to believe in the name of his Son, Jesus Christ, and to love one another as he commanded us."

1 John 4:7: "Dear friends, let us love one another, for love comes from God. Everyone who loves has been born of God and knows God."

1 John 4:11 – 12: "Dear friends, since God so loved us, we also ought to love one another. No one has ever seen God; but if we love one another, God lives in us."

2 John 1:5: "I am not writing you a new command but one we have had from the beginning. I ask that we love one another."

Be devoted to one another.

Romans 12:10: "Be devoted to one another in brotherly love."

Honor one another.

Romans 12:10: "Honor one another above yourselves."

Live in harmony with one another.

Romans 12:16: "Live in harmony with one another. Do not be proud, but be willing to associate with people of low position. Do not be conceited."

1 Thessalonians 5:13: "Live in peace with each other."

1 Peter 3:8: "All of you, live in harmony with one another; be sympathetic, love as brothers, be compassionate and humble."

Stop passing judgment on one another.

Romans 14:13: "Let us stop passing judgment on one another. Instead, make up your mind not to put any stumbling block or obstacle in your brother's way."

Accept one another.

Romans 15:7: "Accept one another, then, just as Christ accepted you, in order to bring praise to God."

Instruct one another.

Romans 15:14: "You yourselves are full of goodness, complete in knowledge and competent to instruct one another."

Colossians 3:16: "Let the word of Christ dwell in you richly as you teach and admonish one another with all wisdom, and as you

sing psalms, hymns and spiritual songs with gratitude in your
hearts to God."

Greet one another with a holy kiss.

Romans 16:16: "Greet one another with a holy kiss. All the
churches of Christ send greetings." (See also 1 Corinthians
16:20; 2 Corinthians 13:12; 1 Peter 5:14.)

Agree with one another.

1 Corinthians 1:10: "I appeal to you, brothers, in the name of our
Lord Jesus Christ, that all of you agree with one another so that
there may be no divisions among you and that you may be perfectly united in mind and thought."

Wait for each other.

1 Corinthians 11:33: "When you come together to eat, wait for each
other."

Have equal concern for each other.

1 Corinthians 12:25: "... so that there should be no division in the
body, but that its parts should have equal concern for each other."

Serve one another.

Galatians 5:13: "You, my brothers, were called to be free. But do not
use your freedom to indulge the sinful nature; rather, serve one
another in love."

Do not provoke or envy one another.

Galatians 5:26: "Let us not become conceited, provoking and envy-
ing each other."

Carry each other's burdens.

Galatians 6:2: "Carry each other's burdens, and in this way you will
fulfill the law of Christ."

Bear with one another.

Ephesians 4:2: "Be completely humble and gentle; be patient, bear-
ing with one another in love."

Colossians 3:13: "Bear with each other and forgive whatever grievances you may have against one another. Forgive as the Lord forgave you."

Be compassionate to one another.

Ephesians 4:32: "Be kind and compassionate to one another."

Forgive one another.

Ephesians 4:32: "... forgiving each other, just as in Christ God forgave you."

Colossians 3:13: "Bear with each other and forgive whatever grievances you may have against one another. Forgive as the Lord forgave you."

Speak to one another with psalms, hymns, and spiritual songs.

Ephesians 5:19: "Speak to one another with psalms, hymns and spiritual songs. Sing and make music in your heart to the Lord."

Submit to one another.

Ephesians 5:21: "Submit to one another out of reverence for Christ."

Do not lie to each other.

Colossians 3:9: "Do not lie to each other, since you have taken off your old self with its practices."

Encourage one another.

1 Thessalonians 4:18: "Encourage each other with these words."

1 Thessalonians 5:11: "Encourage one another."

Hebrews 3:13: "Encourage one another daily, as long as it is called Today, so that none of you may be hardened by sin's deceitfulness."

Hebrews 10:25: "Let us not give up meeting together, as some are in the habit of doing, but let us encourage one another—and all the more as you see the Day approaching."

Build up each other.

1 Thessalonians 5:11: "Build each other up, just as in fact you are doing."

Spur one another on toward love and good deeds.

Hebrews 10:24: "Let us consider how we may spur one another on toward love and good deeds."

Do not give up meeting together.

Hebrews 10:25: "Let us not give up meeting together, as some are in the habit of doing, but let us encourage one another — and all the more as you see the Day approaching."

Do not slander one another.

James 4:11: "Do not slander one another. Anyone who speaks against his brother or judges him speaks against the law and judges it."

Offer hospitality to one another.

1 Peter 4:9: "Offer hospitality to one another without grumbling."

Cloth yourself with humility toward one another.

1 Peter 5:5: "Young men, in the same way be submissive to those who are older. All of you, clothe yourselves with humility toward one another, because, 'God opposes the proud but gives grace to the humble.'"

Be kind to one another.

1 Thessalonians 5:15: "Make sure that nobody pays back wrong for wrong, but always try to be kind to each other and to everyone else."

Don't grumble against one another.

James 5:9: "Don't grumble against each other, brothers, or you will be judged. The Judge is standing at the door!"

Confess your sins to each other.

James 5:16: "Confess your sins to each other."

Pray for each other.

James 5:16: "Pray for each other so that you may be healed. The prayer of a righteous man is powerful and effective."

Study Guide
Follow-up Questions for Each Chapter

This book is best read and discussed as a team. Whether you're on a church governing board, are on a staff leadership team, or have frontline responsibility for spiritual development or small groups, you and your teammates will get a lot more out of it by reading and discussing it together.

The following questions are based on each chapter. They will help you take stock of your current ministry situation as well as dig deeper into the concepts and principles that make for a truly sticky church. They can be used in a variety of ways. You may want to go through them chapter by chapter in a slow and measured pace. Or you may want to simply pick out the best and most helpful questions and use them in a retreat setting to review the entire book at once. Either way, you'll find them beneficial as you work through the practical steps involved in slamming the back door shut or in starting a sermon-based small group ministry within the context of your unique ministry setting.

Part 1: The Sticky Church Advantage

1. Sticky Church

1. Is retention an important value in our church? Why or why not?

2. Many churches have plans and programs to increase the retention level of new believers and visitors, but few are very intentional about long-term retention.

    What are we doing to increase our stickiness with new Christians and visitors?

    Is it working? Why or why not?

    What are we doing to increase our long-term stickiness with those who are already in our church?

    Is it working? Why or why not?

3. Do we have a plan or program in place that measures the size of our back door?

If not, why not?

If we do, how accurate is it? And what does it tell us about the people who are most vulnerable to slipping out the back door?

4. What are the three most effective things we are doing to open the front door?

What are the three most effective things we are doing to close the back door?

2. Who Are These Guys?

1. How do most people who visit our church *hear about* or *find out about* our church?

2. How does the church we are match up to the church we project in our ads and marketing campaigns?

3. When a person or family walks out the back door, are they likely to be noticed, and if so, by whom? What is the likelihood that their leaving will be discussed among our leadership team?

4. What percentage of our average weekend adult attendance is connected to an organized small group? What would be an appropriate percentage for us to aim for, given our current ministry realities?

3. How I Learned about the Importance and Power of Stickiness

1. Which of the following descriptions best describes our church at this time?

A country club (member centered)

An army (task centered)

A recruitment depot (outsider centered)

A movement (goal focused, easy to break into)

A bureaucracy (programmatic, hard to break into)

A _____

2. How do we view the people who are longtime members of our church? Are they treated as tools and resources to be used or as sheep to be cared for?

   If they were asked this question, what would their answer be? Why?

3. Are people in our church being served so well that they want to bring people to church? If so, how so? Or if not, what are we missing?

4. Why Stickier Churches Are Healthier Churches

1. Why do most of our guests and visitors walk through the front door the first time?

   When they come back, what brings them back?

   Do we know for sure?

2. What are our three biggest outreach opportunities during the course of a normal year? (This can be special programming or simply big attendance weekends like Easter.)

   How many new people came last year?

   How many are still with us today?

3. When we have special outreach programs and events, what is the experience of someone who decides to come back the next weekend?

   Is this good or bad? What would be the ideal?

4. Looking at the newest Christians in our church, how did most of them come into a relationship with Jesus? Has it been through our

special programs or through come-and-see invitations to a Bible study or weekend service?

5. How would you grade our current evangelism? Our current follow-up? Our current assimilation?

Part 2: How Small Groups Change Everything

5. Velcroed for Growth

1. How does our church expect people to grow spiritually?

Do we provide a linear set of classes and experiences? If so, which ones seem to work the best, and which ones don't appear to produce much fruit? Why?

How do we accommodate the randomness of most people's spiritual growth?

2. Describe a specific need-to-know or need-to-grow situation you've faced.

3. What opportunities do we provide for people to be velcroed to significant relationships and the Bible?

Are we satisfied with the number of people who have significant relationships centered on the Bible?

What could we do to increase the number?

6. How Small Groups Change Everything

1. Where do small groups fit in the pecking order of our church's ministry? Are they more of an add-on, a key ministry, or something in between?

What percentage of our average adult weekend attendance is in a small group?

What is the participation level of our key staff and lay leaders?

2. How powerful is the Holy Man myth within our ministry? Where does it show up? What are some areas where it's been eradicated?

3. How much sway does the Holy Place myth have within our ministry? Where does it show up? What are some areas where it's been eradicated?

4. When it comes to empowerment and ministry platforms, how many opportunities for significant life-on-life ministry do we offer?

Is this enough?

What percentage of our up-front and key hands-on ministry staff is homegrown? Is this a good thing? Why or why not?

7. Still More Ways That Small Groups Change Everything

1. How does our church rate when it comes to a pattern of honesty and transparency?

What would happen if we set up a sign that read "Marriage Renovation Sign-Ups"?

2. How well are we moving people from good intentions to the actual practice of spiritual disciplines?

Do we have any vehicles in place to help people try out various disciplines to see which ones work best for them?

3. What is the childhood-to-adult cycle in our church? Do we have a way to accurately measure how many children stick as they grow up and how many fade away as young adults?

What are we depending on to make sure that the kids who come to our children's and youth programs will also follow Christ as adults?

8. Making the Message Memorable

1. Osborne claims that the lecture-lab model behind sermon-based small groups provides some powerful educational benefits. Do you agree? Why or why not?

   If you agree, which benefits do you see as being most significant? Why?

   If you disagree, where and why do you think sermon-based groups miss the mark?

2. What percentage of people take notes in our weekend services? And in what other ways do we get them to interact with the sermon both during the message and afterward?

3. What do we do to encourage people to think about and discuss the message after it's delivered?

   Has our entire church ever studied and discussed a sermon series together (for instance, Rick Warren's "Forty Days of Purpose")? If so, what happened?

4. When it comes to basic biblical truth and the tenets of Christian living, where would you put most of the people in our church on the knowledge scale? Why?

   Inspired | Familiar | Bored | Knowledgeable

9. Making the Message Accessible

1. How successful have we been in reeling in the marginally interested who already attend our church?

   What stories do we have of people who started out unmotivated but now have a growing relationship with God?

   What was the ministry, program, or event that God used to bring them to full commitment?

2. How much time does the average person spend in preparation before coming to one of our current small groups?

3. What is the most successful vehicle we have for assimilating new Christians?

How do those without any biblical background or knowledge fit into our current small group structures? How high would their intimidation factor be?

High | Medium | Low

4. What are the primary skills a leader needs in order to be successful within our current small group model?

Part 3: Sermon-Based Small Groups

10. Why Some Groups Jell and Some Don't

1. What is the ideal size of a small group in our ministry context? Why?

2. Do you agree that there are significant differences between small groups made up primarily of married couples and small groups made up entirely of men, women, or singles? Why or why not?

3. Which of our small groups are stickiest?

Which ones have the greatest turnover?

In what ways does the size or makeup of our small groups contribute to their stickiness or high turnover rate?

4. What are some potential station-in-life groupings and special-interest groupings that exist in our church and could be utilized to provide the foundation for deeper friendships?

5. Osborne contends that people are like Legos and describes the impact this similarity can have on the level of connectedness

within a small group. Do you agree or disagree with his analysis? Why or why not?

6. Do we have new groups for new people?

7. Do we currently ask our small groups to divide in order to allow for church growth? If so, are we experiencing any unintended consequences because of it?

11. Flies on the Wall

1. How do the basic elements of Osborne's sermon-based small groups (refreshments, sharing, study and discussion, prayer, worship, and service) match up with or differ from what we currently do in our small groups?

Are there any elements we should add or would not want to have?

Are there any that are out of balance, either overemphasized or neglected?

2. Which of the three types of questions (Getting to Know Me, Into the Bible, and Application) do we do best? Which do we do worst?

Which ones do you like best? Least?

3. Do the people in our small groups feel the freedom to digress from the assigned topic(s)?

Are people free to disagree with the party line?

4. What role do we want worship and service projects to play in our small group ministry? How much freedom should we allow? Why?

12. Overcoming the Time Crunch

1. What are some of the ways in which our leaders and small groups are impacted by the time crunch? Be as specific as possible.

2. North Coast Church assumes that the average person has only two time slots per week that they can (or will) give to ministry. How does that fit with our congregation and community?

3. Do you think it's a good thing or a bad thing to adapt to the time pressures of the culture? Why?

4. If cutting the competition is an important part of increasing congregational involvement in small groups, what are the major sources of ministry competition that our small groups face?

   Is there anything that should or can be changed to remove or reduce the competition?

   In light of our current sources of ministry competition, what is a realistic goal for our percentage of congregational involvement in small groups?

5. How much time does it take to be a member of a small group in our church? How much time does it take to be a small group leader?

   In light of our current ministry structures, how reasonable is it to expect lay leaders and board members to also participate in or lead a small group?

   Is this acceptable? Why or why not?

13. Determining Your Primary Purpose

1. What would most of the people in one of our small groups say the purpose of their small group is?

   How well does this match up with what our leadership would describe as the primary purpose?

2. How does our church measure success or failure in making disciples?

   How are we doing?

How do our measurements differ from those used by North Coast Church?

3. What standards or vital signs do we currently use to measure the health of our church?

How are we doing?

How do our measurements differ from the five vital signs used by North Coast Church?

4. Are there any areas of our small group ministry that have experienced (or are in danger of experiencing) significant mission creep? Be specific.

If so, what should or can be done?

14. Entry Points and Escape Routes

1. How easy is it to join one of our small groups?

How easy is it to get out of one of our small groups?

2. What is the length of commitment we ask someone to make before they join a small group?

What impact does this have on people's willingness to sign up for a group?

How does this impact the "weasel factor" in our small groups?

3. How easy are we making it for people who have an initial negative experience with a small group to try another one?

Do we have a way to measure how many people try one group and never try another?

Do we know how many try out multiple groups before settling into one?

15. Why Dividing Groups Is a Dumb Idea

1. Do you agree that dividing groups is a dumb idea? Why or why not?

2. How do most people in our small groups feel about dividing groups as a growth strategy?

3. Osborne talks about groups that are friendly but no longer have the relational or emotional capacity to connect with new members. Have you ever been in such a group?

   If so, what happened?

4. Do you think the concept of Mayberry in San Diego is a spiritually healthy idea or a recipe for spiritually stagnant relationships? Why?

16. Finding and Developing Leaders

1. Do you agree that every organization eventually becomes a direct reflection of its leadership, whether for good or for bad? Why or why not?

2. How successful have we been at finding the "right kind of leaders"?

   What traits have proven to be most important in the recruitment of successful small group leaders?

   Are there any traits that have proven to be an indicator that some-one will not be a good small group leader within our system?

3. How do you respond to Osborne's list of traits to avoid? Which ones do you most agree and disagree with — and why?

4. What has been our experience when asking for volunteers to lead a group? Has it been mostly good or mostly bad? Why?

5. Do we ever scare off leaders by raising the bar of expectations too high too fast? Why or why not?

17. Training Leaders

1. How would our small group leaders describe their training?

Inadequate | Adequate | Just Right | A Little Too Much | Overload

2. Do you agree that there is a fundamental disconnect in the way that staff and lay leaders tend to view extra meetings?

3. How much effort does it take to get our leaders to show up for training? What, if anything, does that tell us about our current training process?

4. Are there any ways in which we could make our leadership training more accessible and desirable?

Are there any parts of the process that could be time-shifted or made more bite-sized?

5. How do our rookie leaders and our veteran leaders differ?

How should this impact their training?

18. Why Cho's Model Didn't Work in Your Church

1. How many times have we reengineered or relaunched our small group ministry?

2. What impact has Cho's model had on our small group ministry over the years? What parts of his model have shown up in our thinking and values?

3. Do you agree with Osborne's analysis of the key differences between the cultures where Cho's model works and the ones where it doesn't?

What rings most true to you?

What doesn't?

4. How effective have our small groups been in reaching non-Christians for Christ and bringing them into the fellowship of the church?

19. Before You Start

1. How well do our small group methods align with our small group vision? Be specific.

2. Who are we primarily trying to reach with our small groups?

   Does everyone on our leadership team agree with that goal?

3. Using the small group funnel, how does what we do in our small groups match up with who we see as our primary target?

4. Which of the three discipleship and leadership training models most resonates with you personally?

   Which one best fits the philosophy and DNA of our church?

5. Where have we turned for help in developing or fine-tuning our small group model—to the best models out there or to churches that fit well with our unique culture and values? Explain.

Notes

1. Matthew 28:18 – 20.
2. Mark 4:1 – 20.
3. See 1 Peter 2:4 – 10; 1 Timothy 2:5; Matthew 27:50 – 51.
4. Acts 17:11.
5. See 2 Samuel 16:5 – 13 for David's story.
6. See 1 Corinthians 9:19 – 22, where Paul speaks of becoming all things to all people so he might win some.
7. Matthew 12:20.
8. Masterplanninggroup.com.
9. C. S. Lewis, *The Screwtape Letters* (New York: Macmillan, 1975), 35.
10. David Yonggi Cho, *Successful Home Cell Groups* (South Plainfield, NJ: Bridge-Logos Publishers, 1981).

About the Leadership Network Innovation Series

Since 1984, Leadership Network has fostered church innovation and growth by diligently pursuing its far-reaching mission statement: *To identify high-capacity Christian leaders, to connect them with other leaders, and to help them multiply their impact.*

While specific techniques may vary as the church faces new opportunities and challenges, Leadership Network consistently focuses on bringing together entrepreneurial leaders who are pursuing similar ministry initiatives. The resulting peer-to-peer interaction, dialogue, and collaboration—often across denominational lines—helps these leaders better refine their individual strategies and accelerate their own innovations.

To further enhance this process, Leadership Network develops and distributes highly targeted ministry tools and resources, including books, DVDs and videotapes, special reports, e-publications, and free downloads.

Launched in 2006, the Leadership Network Innovation Series presents case studies and insights from leading practitioners and pioneering churches that are successfully navigating the ever-changing streams of spiritual renewal in modern society. Each book offers *real* stories, about *real* leaders, in *real* churches, doing *real* ministry. Readers gain honest and thorough analyses, transferable principles, and clear guidance on how to put proven ideas to work in their individual settings.

With the assistance of Leadership Network—and the Leadership Network Innovation Series—today's Christian leaders are energized, equipped, inspired, and enabled to multiply their own dynamic kingdom-building initiatives. And the pace of innovative ministry is growing as never before.

For additional information on the mission or activities of Leadership Network, please contact:

LEADERSHIP ✖ NETWORK®
innovation series

800-765-5323 • www.leadnet.org • client.care@leadnet.org

The Unity Factor, 4th Edition

By Larry Osborne

Published by OWL'S NEST
ISBN 978-0-9708186-1-4

Healthy leadership teams are no accident. In this classic, Larry Osborne provides church leaders with no-nonsense wisdom and real-life solutions for getting everyone on the same page—and perhaps more important, keeping them there over the long haul. Let Larry show you the secrets for developing and maintaining a truly unified and healthy leadership team.

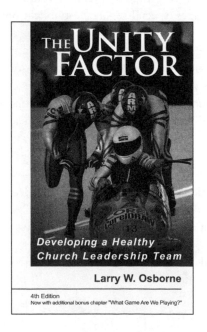

Available at www.northcoastchurch.com
and fine bookstores everywhere

What Others Are Saying about *The Unity Factor*

This book could save your church from needless conflict and division. Listen and learn from it!

—Rick Warren, Pastor and author
Saddleback Church, Lake Forest, California

Larry Osborne's message will save a pastor years of frustration with his veteran insights. He's "been there and done that" with leaders. He has helped me more than once to clarify my leadership strategy. His life and church are living proof he knows what he's talking about!

—Steve Sjogren, Church planter and author

I loved *The Unity Factor* when I first read it several years ago. Few books become more relevant as they age. But Larry's wisdom on leadership is more helpful to me now than ever. Its clarity and simplicity cut through the glut of contemporary punditry. My hope is that a fresh generation of readers will find new direction in this updated version.

—Bill Hull, Pastor and author

Larry writes like a wise mentor, sharing his profoundly simple proven approach to getting your team to work together without splits, shouting matches, or a "range war board." If you are a pastor, consider rereading this book once a year for the rest of your life.

—Bobb Biehl, President
Masterplanning Group International

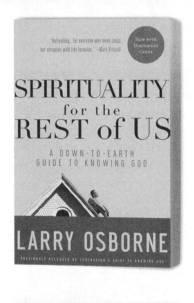

The Leadership Network Innovation Series

Leadership from the Inside Out
Examining the Inner Life of a Healthy Church Leader

Kevin Harney

Kevin Harney writes, "The vision of this book is to assist leaders as they discover the health, wisdom, and joy of living an examined life. It is also to give practical tools for self-examination." Sharing stories and wisdom from his years in ministry, Harney shows you how to maintain the most powerful tool in your leadership toolbox: YOU. Your heart, so you can love well. Your mind, so you can continue to learn and grow. Your ears, your eyes, your mouth. Consider this your essential guide to conducting your own complete interior health exam, so you can spot and fix any problems, preserve the things that matter most, and grow as a source of vision, strength, and hope to others.

Softcover: 978-0-310-25943-5

The Leadership Network Innovation Series

The Big Idea
Focus the Message—Multiply the Impact

Dave Ferguson, Jon Ferguson, and Eric Bramlett

The Big Idea can help you creatively present one laser-focused theme each week to be discussed in families and small groups.

The Big Idea shows how to engage in a process of creative collaboration that brings people together and maximizes missional impact.

The Big Idea can energize a church staff and bring alignment and focus to many diverse church ministries.

This book shows how the Big Idea has helped Community Christian Church better accomplish the Jesus mission and reach thousands of people in nine locations and launch a church-planting network with partner churches across the country.

Softcover: 978-0-310-27241-0